30 00

Justice Louis D. Brandeis

Justice Louis D. Brandeis:

A Bibliography of Writings and Other Materials on the Justice

Gene Teitelbaum

Professor of Law
University of Louisville

FRED B. ROTHMAN & CO.
Littleton, Colorado 80127

1988

Cataloging-in-Publication Data

TEITELBAUM, GENE.
 Justice Louis D. Brandeis : a bibliography of writings and other
 materials on the justice / by Gene Teitelbaum.

  p.   cm.
 ISBN 0-8377-1215-7
 1. Brandeis, Louis Dembitz, 1856–1941—Bibliography.   2. Law—
United States—Bibliography.   I. Title.
KF213.B68T45 1987
016.34773'26—dc19
[B]
[016.3473073534]   87-25962
[B]   CIP

Printed in the United States of America

Contents

Introduction

Louis D. Brandeis had four successful careers: he was a skilled practising attorney; he was a leader in the late nineteenth century and early twentieth century American reform movement for the social and economic betterment of the working class; he was the most visible and famous American Jew and the leader of the American Zionist movement for many years; and he served as an Associate Justice of the Supreme Court of the United States. Brandeis was nominated to the high court by President Wilson in 1916 at the age of sixty. His nomination was confirmed by the United States Senate after a long and bitter battle. He served on the bench for twenty-three years, resigning in 1939. During that period, he and Justice Oliver Wendell Holmes were the torchbearers of the liberal cause. The *Washington Post* headline announcing Brandeis' death described his judicial tenure succinctly and accurately in these words, "Lived to See Dissenting Liberalism Vindicated."

In the last few years, there has been a resurgence in interest about the Justice. Several full-length, scholarly biographies have been written about him, and his letters that previously were only found in research libraries, have been made more available. The two largest collections of his letters, in the Harvard Law School Library and University of Louisville Law Library, have been microfilmed and are available for sale. In addition, Professors Melvin I. Urofsky and David W. Levy have compiled a five-volume collection of the most representative Brandeis letters.[1]

This bibliography contains all the major and nearly all of the shorter materials written about Justice Brandeis since 1957. To enable

---

1. Melvin I. Urofsky and David W. Levy, eds., *Letters of Louis D. Brandeis* (Albany: State University of New York Press, 1971–1978).

the user to gauge the length of each item, the first and last page of each entry has been noted. Extremely short articles of little significance have been excluded as have items published for very limited distribution or in local publications. To aid the researcher, the vast majority of the entries are annotated. The annotations are relatively short because, in most instances, the title of an entry sufficiently describes its contents. All but a handful of the entries portray Brandeis in a positive light.

Professor Roy M. Mersky's earlier bibliography[2] of writings by and about Justice Brandeis is the starting point for this publication. Instead of reinventing the wheel by listing all pre-1957 entries, the reader is referred to Professor Mersky's work. Pre-1957 items not included in the Mersky work are included in this publication.

This bibliography is organized into ten chapters. The first chapter covers books where Brandeis is the sole or major subject.

The second chapter is devoted to law review and legal periodical articles on the Justice. Because of their depth of coverage and extensive bibliographic footnotes, this grouping has been placed second. For the most part, book reviews of biographies of Brandeis have been excluded unless the review itself or the reviewer is significant. A major exception to this policy are book reviews of Bruce Murphy's 1982 joint biography of Brandeis and Felix Frankfurter.[3] Murphy's work unleashed a torrent of reviews, especially in law reviews and legal periodicals, with some reviewers openly hostile to his book, but with most reviewers finding some validity in his thesis. Book reviews are listed under the reviewer's name. A few important book reviews that appeared in non-legal periodicals are included in chapter five.

The third chapter entitled "Partials of Books" contains entries where Brandeis is discussed as part of a larger topic or biography. Because Brandeis' influence on American life was extraordinary and far reaching it would have been impossible to examine and list every book which could have been included in this section. That being the case, coverage in this section is selective.

Chapter 4 entitled "Essays" contains articles on the Justice which were written by one author and published in a collection of essays edited by another person. The fifth chapter is a collection of non-legal periodical articles, which were written for either a scholarly or a popular

---

2. Roy M. Mersky, *Louis Dembitz Brandeis, 1856–1941, A Bibliography*, Yale Law Library Publications No. 15 (New Haven, Conn.: Yale Law School, 1958), 44 pp. Reprinted in 1987 and available from Fred B. Rothman & Co., 10368 West Centennial Road, Littleton, Colorado 80127.

3. Bruce Allen Murphy, *The Brandeis/Frankfurter Connection: The Secret Political Activities of Two Supreme Court Justices* (New York: Oxford University Press, 1982).

audience. Many of these entries chronicle Brandeis' Jewish and Zionist activities.

Chapter 6 "Correspondence to and from Brandeis, in Manuscript Collections" is a large and important segment of this work. Although the entries found in the previous sections are readily available throughout the country, letters, by their very nature, can only be found and examined in the library owning the letter. Professor Mersky's bibliography lists only those Brandeis letters in the Yale University Law library. Coverage in this bibliography attempts to be comprehensive in order to enable the reader to be exposed to the breadth of Brandeis' interests and wide circle of correspondents.

Speeches by Brandeis are included in chapter 7. This chapter expands on Professor Mersky's work due to the fact that in the last few years new and additional information concerning the Justice's speeches has surfaced. Many references to Brandeis' speeches are found in his scrapbooks that are housed in the Brandeis Collection at the University of Louisville Law Library. "Speeches about Brandeis" are found in Chapter 8. Speeches that were not published or were only printed in an abridged format are included. Chapter 9 "Miscellany" contains items that did not fit into the other categories.

In the tenth and final chapter, "Sources Used and Guide for Further Research," both the libraries and the materials used in compiling this work are identified and sources (books, indexes, people and topics) for additional study and research on the Justice are set forth.

Updating for this bibliography is planned so that items published after 1986 and material that has been overlooked will be included.

A work of this type can never be accomplished without the assistance of others. I would like to thank all the librarians who answered my requests for information and direction. The help of Sharon Mills, Sandy Hartz and others in Academic and Professional Development Services of the University of Louisville is particularly appreciated. They deciphered my handwriting, produced this coherent work, and made all the necessary additions and corrections graciously, accurately and with dispatch.

GENE TEITELBAUM

Chronology

1856. Born on November 13th in Louisville, Kentucky to Adolph and Frederika Dembitz Brandeis.

1872-1875. After attending public school in Louisville, went to Europe and studied at the Annen-Realschule in Dresden, Germany.

1875-1878. Entered Harvard Law School, without first attending college. Graduated in 1877 with a LL.B. degree. Spent the next academic year, 1877-78, in graduate study at Harvard Law School.

1878. Moved to St. Louis, Missouri, where he practiced law for one year.

1879. Returned to Boston, to practice law there until 1916. Was in partnership with Samuel Warren as Warren & Brandeis, Esqs. until 1889. The partnership was dissolved when Warren died, however, the firm's name remained the same until 1897. The law firm of Brandeis, Dunbar & Nutter was founded in 1897.

1880s. Started a career of being involved in various civic reform movements in Boston. Later, became active on the national scene in the reform movement.

1890. With Warren, wrote the famous law review article, "The Right to Privacy," which was published in the *Harvard Law Review*, vol. 4, p. 193-220 (1890).

1891. Married Alice Goldmark on March 23rd.

1893. His first daughter, Susan, was born on February 27th.

1896. His second daughter, Elizabeth, was born on April 25th.

1905. Became involved in insurance matters. Introduced the concept of savings bank life insurance, which after some opposition has become an integral part of savings bank services.

1908. On January 15th, argued the case of *Muller v. Oregon* before the United States Supreme Court. Revolutionized legal brief writing by using non-legal materials extensively in his brief. The case was decided in his favor on February 24th, 208 U.S. 412.

1910. Became active in the New York City garment industry, first as a mediator of the workers' strike, then as an arbitrator, from 1910–1914. His 1910 Protocol brought industrial peace to the industry.

1910. Served as counsel for *Collier's Weekly* in the Ballinger-Pinchot investigation conducted by the U.S. Senate. Although he lost the investigation, he won the "war" as Secretary of the Interior Ballinger resigned soon thereafter.

1910. Made his first public comments on the issue of Zionism on December 9th. Started to become active in Zionist affairs.

1912. Joined the American Zionist movement.

1914–1916. Served as Chairman of the Provisional Committee for General Zionist Affairs.

1916. Nominated by President Woodrow Wilson on January 28th to become an Associate Justice of the Supreme Court of the United States, replacing the deceased Joseph R. Lamar. A long and bitter confirmation struggle ensued. Finally, on June 1st, his nomination was confirmed by the U.S. Senate by a vote of 47 to 22, with 29 abstentions. Was sworn in on June 5th, five months prior to his sixtieth birthday.

1917. Helped formulate the Balfour Declaration.

1920. Attended the World Zionist Organization's conference in London, England, in July. Lost the fight with Chaim Weizmann over the direction Zionism should take.

1921. Attended the Zionist Organization of America's conference in Cleveland, Ohio, on June 5–7. After losing the fight, he and many others resigned their positions in the organization.

1927. Wrote his now famous concurrence in *Whitney v. California*, 274 U.S. 357, 372.

1928. Dissented in *Olmstead v. United States*, 277 U.S. 438, 471.

1936. Celebrated his eightieth birthday.

1938. Wrote the landmark decision on civil procedure. *Erie Railroad Co. v. Tompkins,* 304 U.S. 64.

1939. Resigned from the U.S. Supreme Court on February 13th; was succeeded by William O. Douglas.

1941. Died in Washington, D.C. on October 5th, after having a stroke several days earlier.

1945. His wife, Alice, died on October 12th. Both were cremated and are interred at the School of Law, University of Louisville, Louisville, Kentucky.

CHAPTER 1

Books and Pamphlets about Brandeis

Baker, Leonard. *Brandeis and Frankfurter: A Dual Biography*. New York: Harper & Row, Publishers, 1984. 567 pp. Interviews conducted (26), manuscript collections consulted and oral history recordings used, pp. 495-499; bibliography, pp. 499-508.

Berg, Alan Lee. *A Union of the Spirit: The Jewish Transformation of Louis Brandeis*. M.A. thesis (Rabbinic). Cincinnati: Hebrew Union College, 1973. 56 pp., typescript. Notes, pp. 48-53; bibliography, pp. 54-56.

Borovitz, Neal. *The Brandeis-Weizmann Conflict—"An Analysis of The Causal Factors."* Term paper. Cincinnati: Hebrew Union College, 1972. 37 pp., typescript.

Borovitz traces the events which lead to the Brandeis-Weizmann split and their three-year long conflict.

The Brandeis Avukah Annual of 1932. A Collection of Essays on Contemporary Zionist Thought Dedicated to Justice Louis D. Brandeis. Edited by Joseph Shalom Shubow. New York: Avukah, American Student Zionist Federation, 1932. 808 pp.

Pages 1-20 contain nineteen short tributes to Brandeis. *The Brandeis Avukah of 1936* is identical to the 1932 volume because this volume was reprinted in 1936 to celebrate Brandeis' eightieth birthday.

Brandeis, Louis Dembitz. *Letters of Louis D. Brandeis*. 5 vol. Edited by Melvin I. Urofsky and David W. Levy. Albany: State University of New York Press, 1971-1978. Vol. 1, *Urban Reformer, 1870-1907*, 610 pp.; Vol. 2, *People's Attorney, 1907-1912*, 750 pp.; Vol. 3, *Progressive and Zionist, 1913-1915*, 705 pp.; Vol. 4, *Mr. Justice Brandeis, 1916-1921*, 587 pp.; Vol. 5, *Elder Statesman, 1921-1941*, 770 pp.

Professors Urofsky and Levy examined the Brandeis Papers at the University of Louisville Law Library and selected the most representative letters. They also used letters from other manuscript collections and individuals. There is a cumulative index in volume 5, as well as a "Cumulative Key to Letter Source Citations," vol. 5, xxiii–xxix.

The editors, besides selecting the most representative Brandeis letters, have annotated them by including a vast amount of information about the persons referred to and events in the footnotes that follow the letters.

Caminker, Harold Floyd. *The Weizmann–Brandeis Fight 1920–1921: What Happened and Why.* Term paper. Cincinnati: Hebrew Union College, 1977. 19 pp., typescript.

Cowett, Mark. *Louis D. Brandeis (1856–1912).* Honors thesis. Appleton, [Wisc.?]: Lawrence University, June 1973. 77 leaves, typescript. Bibliography, 6 unnumbered pages at the end.

Cowett describes Brandeis' life to 1912. He tries to show the elitist and democratic elements in Brandeis' life, his career and ideas in light of the Progressive Era.

Dawson, Nelson Lloyd. *Louis D. Brandeis, Felix Frankfurter, and the New Deal.* Ph.D. diss. Lexington: University of Kentucky, 1975. 397 pp.

———, *Louis D. Brandeis, Felix Frankfurter, and the New Deal.* Hamden, Conn.: Archon Books, 1980. 272 pp. Notes, pp. 179–250; bibliography, pp. 251–265; manuscript and oral history sources, p. 251.

DeLong, Jane Jebb Mansbridge. *Brandeis and Sutherland—Apostles of Individualism.* Ph.D. diss. Cambridge, Mass.: Harvard University, 1971. 593 leaves. Bibliography, pp. 582–593.

Drushal, John Garber. *The Speeches of Louis Dembitz Brandeis, 1908–1916.* Ph.D. diss. Columbus: Ohio State University, 1951, 527 pp., typescript. Footnotes are at the end of each chapter; bibliography, pp. 301–312.

This work examines Brandeis as a public speaker by analyzing six of Brandeis' major speeches; they are reprinted in the appendices. This work is available from University Microfilms International.

Elmes, Cecil Frederick. *O'Fallon Decision and the Brandeis Dissent....* Chicago: Cecil F. Elmes Organization, 1929, 22 pp.

In *St. Louis & O'Fallon Railway Co. v. United States,* 279 U.S. 461 (1929), the Supreme Court reversed the Interstate Commerce Commission's Order that set aside a freight rate because it did not use the proper criteria. Brandeis dissented and wrote an especially long opinion (pp. 488–548). Justices Holmes and Stone joined him in dissent.

Everson, Cora Eva. *Brandeis: Our Liberal Judge. . . .* M.A. thesis. Columbus: Ohio State University, 1936. 68 leaves. Bibliography, pp. 64-68.

Ewbank, Barbara Harris. *The Non-Zionist Zionism of Louis Brandeis.* 1973. 18 pp., typescript.

Ewbank traces Brandeis' commitment to Zionism during the time period 1912-1921. Brandeis left the movement after being soundly beaten at the Cleveland convention of American Zionists over the direction Zionism should take.

I found this monograph in the American Jewish Archives' near-print Brandeis file. It does not indicate where it was issued.

Fraenkel, Josef. *Louis D. Brandeis (1856-1941) Patriot, Judge and Zionist.* London: Education Committee of the Hillel Foundation, 1959. 24 pp. Bibliography, p. 24. It is number two in the series "Makers of Modern Jewish History."

Frank, David. *Louis D. Brandeis As a Jew.* Term paper. Cincinnati: Hebrew Union College, 1974. 11 pp., typescript.

After recounting Brandeis' decision to become active in American Jewish life, Frank concludes that there is not one person or event that fully accounts for Brandeis' conversion and that Brandeis was sincere in his new belief, rather than making a mere opportunistic gesture.

Gal, Allon. *Brandeis of Boston.* Cambridge, Mass.: Harvard University Press, 1980. 271 pp. Bibliography, pp. 209-217; notes, pp. 219-261; manuscript collections, scrapbooks consulted and interviews conducted (36), pp. 209-211.

Brandeis lived almost forty years in Boston. Gal traces that period in Brandeis' life and career.

————, *Brandeis, Progressivism and Zionism: A Study in the Interaction of Ideas and Social Background.* Ph.D. diss. Waltham, Mass.: Brandeis University, 1975. 633 pp., typescript. Notes, pp. 553-613; bibliography, pp. 614-633; manuscript and scrapbook collections consulted and interviews conducted (33), pp. 614-617. This work is available from University Microfilms International.

Gans, Albert W., and Robert Oppenheimer, eds. *Louis Dembitz Brandeis.* 1957. 8 pp., softcover. "This pamphlet has been prepared for use in conjunction with the Brandeis exhibit at Temple B'rith Kodesh, [Rochester, New York] in February, 1957."

This work contains four short articles on Brandeis: Alfred W. Gans, "Brandeis, a Lawyer's Appreciation"; an excerpt from Charles E.

Wyzanski's 1956 *Atlantic Monthly* article, "Brandeis"; Philip S. Bernstein, "The Brandeis I Knew"; and Meyer Jacobstein, "A Rochester Memory." In addition, it has a reprint of Brandeis' speech, "The Jewish Problem and How to Solve It."

Geller, Stuart Mitchell. *Louis Dembitz Brandeis and Zionism.* Thesis (Rabbinic). Cincinnati: Hebrew Union College, 1970. 134 pp., typescript. Bibliography, pp. 131–134.

The author's thesis is that Brandeis became a Zionist because of his conviction, not out of political opportunism.

Grand, Tamar. *Louis Dembitz Brandeis. Illustrations . . . Prepared by William Steinel. . . .* New York: Histadruth Ivrith of America; Montreal: Canadian Association for Hebrew Education and Culture, 1967. 26 pp., softcover.

The work is written for juveniles. It was prepared for use with the color filmstrip "Louis D. Brandeis, Giant of Justice and Champion of Zion."

Harris, Barbara Ann. *Zionist Speeches of Louis Dembitz Brandeis: A Critical Edition.* Ph.D. diss. in Speech. Los Angeles: University of California at Los Angeles, 1967 (c1968). 504 pp., typescript. Bibliography, pp. 469–475; list of Brandeis' Zionist speeches (31), pp. 479–480. Harris lists the archives, interviews (4) and correspondence she had while working on this dissertation, pp. 474–475. This work is available from University Microfilms International.

Jacobson, Janice Mark. *Mr. Justice Brandeis on Regulation and Competition: An Analysis of His Economic Opinions.* Ph.D. diss. in Political Science. New York: Columbia University, 1973. 338 pp., typescript. Bibliography, pp. 328–329; cases, pp. 329–338.

Brandeis was always a staunch foe of monopolies. Jacobson investigates his economic philosophy.

Jewish Agency for Palestine. *Minutes of the Meeting in Memory of Mr. Louis D. Brandeis.* October 15, 1941. 8 pp., typescript.

It is a series of eulogies of Brandeis that were delivered at the afternoon session of the Zionist Action Committee of the Jewish Agency.

The Jewish Club, Inc., New York. *The Ten-Year Book of the Jewish Club, Respectfully Dedicated to Mr. Justice Louis D. Brandeis on the Occasion of His Eighty-Third Birthday Anniversary, November 13, 1939.* New York, 1939. 104 pp.

Only the first thirty pages relate to Justice Brandeis. The remainder of the book contains materials relating to the Club and advertisements solicited for the dinner honoring Brandeis, which was held at the Waldorf-Astoria Hotel in New York City on November 12th.

The three major tributes are: Abraham H. Cohen, "For a Blessing to All Men" (pp. 11-13); Charles Evans Hughes, *A Tribute* (pp. 19-20); and Horace M. Kallen, "The Incarnation of the Idealism of America" (pp. 25-27).

Jewish Congress Organization Committee. *To the Jews of America—The Jewish Congress Versus The American Jewish Committee. A Complete Statement with the Correspondence Between Louis D. Brandeis and Cyrus Adler.* New York, August 1915. 22 pp.

Adler is an almost forgotten figure today. In the beginning of the twentieth century, he was a prominent Jewish leader. He represented the American Jewish Committee at the Paris Peace Conference, 1918-1919. Although not a Zionist, Adler thought of Palestine as the birthplace of his religious heritage.

Kallen, Horace Meyer. *The Faith of Louis D. Brandeis, Zionist.* New York: Hadassah, The Women's Zionist Organization of America, Inc., 1943. 34 pp., softcover. Foreword by Rose G. Jacobs, pp. 1-4.

The booklet describes Brandeis' entire life. It was reprinted in Kallen's *"Of Them Which Say They Are Jews; and Other Essays on the Jewish Struggle for Survival,"* at pp. 131-153. Edited by Judah Pilch. New York: Bloch Publishing Co., 1954. 242 pp.

Levy, Eugene H. *Gus Karger: Taft, The Jews and Brandeis: Correspondence Between William Howard Taft and Gus Karger: 1907-1924.* Term paper. Cincinnati: Hebrew Union College, 1971. 22 pp., typescript.

Gus Karger was the Washington, D.C. correspondent for the *Cincinnati Times-Star* for many years, 1906 to 1924.

Louis D. Brandeis Colony in Palestine. *America's Tribute.* June 17, 1942. 24 pp.

It contains twelve short addresses (not listed separately herein) on Brandeis, delivered at a dinner at the Hotel Commodore, New York City. The group's purpose was to form a colony in Israel for refugees.

Louisville. University. School of Law. *Brandeis as Jurist: Craftsmanship with Inspiration.* Louisville, Ky., 1965. 18 pp., softcover.

The work contains the two speeches given on January 26 and 27, 1965, at the first annual "Mr. Justice Brandeis and the Growth of American Law" lecture series. Professor Walter Brandeis Raushenbush (his grandson) gave the lecture entitled "Brandeis As Jurist: Craftsmanship with Inspiration" (pp. 1-16). Also, Dr. Maurice R. R. Davies spoke. His talk entitled "A British Appreciation and Tribute to Mr. Justice Brandeis" is printed at pp. 17-18.

Louisville. University. School of Law. Student Bar Association. *Fiftieth Anniversary Convocation of Justice Brandeis' Appointment to the Supreme Court of the United States.* Louisville, Ky., January 28, 1966. 20 pp., typescript.

Professor Louis L. Jaffe gave the major speech, "Was Brandeis An Activist?" (pp. 6-20). In addition, short tributes were delivered by Willard Hurst, Samuel H. Maslon and Paul A. Freund. All four men are former Brandeis law clerks.

Luney, Kenneth Dean. *Mr. Justice Brandeis and The Problems of Labor.* Ph.D. diss. in Economics. Urbana: University of Illinois, 1932. 179 pp., typescript. Bibliography, pp. 165-179.

Luney discusses Brandeis' philosophy and role in the labor movement, both before and after he became a Justice of the United States Supreme Court. [Mersky, at page 29, listed only the "Abstract" of this work.]

McLean, George. *The Valuation of Public Utilities. Criticism of the Recent Minority Opinion of Justice Brandeis of the Supreme Court of the United States.* Dubuque, Iowa, 1923. 12 pp.

Murphy, Bruce Allen. *The Brandeis/Frankfurter Connection: The Secret Political Activities of Two Supreme Court Justices.* New York: Oxford University Press, 1982. 473 pp., Notes, pp. 365-452; bibliography, pp. 454-466; manuscripts and oral history, pp. 454-456; interviews (22), pp. 456.

This is a highly critical biography of the two Justices. The book's publication caused a flood of book reviews. The legal ones are listed in this work in chapter 2, "Law Review and Legal Periodical Articles," under the name of the reviewer, non-law ones in chapter 5, "Non-Legal Periodical Articles," under the name of the reviewer. For additional non-law book reviews, see *Book Review Digest* 1982 at p. 950, and 1983 at p. 1042, for summaries of other published reviews. The word count of each review is given. Also, consult *Book Review Index,* 1982 Cumulation at p. 369, 1983 Cumulation at p. 385, and 1984 Cumulation at p. 509.

————, *Supreme Court Justices as Politicians: The Extra Judicial Activities of Justices Louis D. Brandeis and Felix Frankfurter.* Ph.D. diss. Charlottesville: University of Virginia, 1978.

National Committee for the Louis D. Brandeis Memorial Colony in Palestine. *Proceedings of the Dinners, June 23 and 24, 1943.* New York City and Chicago. 48 pp.

Prints twenty-two addresses, messages and resolutions of varying length, but most are short, praising Justice Brandeis. The cover reads, "Toward Fulfillment of the Brandeis Vision." Supreme Court Justice Robert Jackson spoke. His speech is printed at pp. 20–26 and was reprinted in popular magazines, *see* chapter 5, "Non-Legal Periodical Articles," *infra.*

Newland, Chester A. *See* chapter 5, "Non-Legal Periodical Articles."

Noble, Iris. *Firebrand for Justice: A Biography of Louis Dembitz Brandeis.* Philadelphia: Westminister Press, 1969. 176 pp. Bibliography, pp. 169–170.

It is an uncomplicated biography of Brandeis.

Oglio, Donna Marianne. *The American Reformer: Psychological and Sociological Origins: A Comparative Study of Jane Addams, Louis Dembitz Brandeis, and William Jennings Bryan.* Ph.D. diss. in Political Science. New York: City University of New York, 1979. 401 pp., typescript. Footnotes on Brandeis, pp. 242–250; bibliography on Brandeis, pp. 395–397.

Chapter 3 is entitled "The Youth of Louis Dembitz Brandeis: Legal Reformer" (pp. 162–250). This work is available from University Microfilms International.

Palestine Economic Corporation. *Proceedings of the Louis D. Brandeis Memorial Meeting Held Under the Auspices of the Palestine Economic Corporation at Ein Hashofet, October 16, 1941.* Various paginations, typescript.

The work contains eleven short speeches (not listed individually herein) that were delivered at that meeting, which was a eulogy to Brandeis.

Palestine on Brandeis. Some Tributes to Mr. Justice Louis D. Brandeis on the Occasion of His 80th Birthday, November 11, 1936. Spoken or Written by Leading Members of the Jewish Community in Palestine. Jerusalem, 1937. 38, 38 pp.

Contains ten tributes (not listed individually herein) to the Justice. Each is printed in both Hebrew and in English.

Paper, Lewis J. *Brandeis.* Englewood Cliffs, N.J.: Prentice-Hall, Inc., 1983. 442 pp. Notes and sources, pp. 403–432; interviews conducted (36), p. 400.

This is a popular biography of Brandeis. Mr. Paper humanizes him.

Peare, Catherine Owens. *The Louis D. Brandeis Story.* New York: Thomas Y. Crowell Company, 1970. 297 pp. Bibliography, pp. 282–288; "Suggestions for Further Readings," p. 280.

Pennington, Leslie T. *Louis Brandeis, A Light on the Path of the Just.* (Series xiv, no. 13.) A sermon preached by Rev. Leslie T. Pennington in the First

Church in Cambridge (Unitarian). Cambridge, Mass.: Post Office Mission, [1941?]. 12 pp., softcover.

This work is a glowing tribute to the Justice, given a short time before Brandeis died.

Rabinowitz, Ezekiel. *Justice Louis D. Brandeis: The Zionist Chapter of His Life.* New York: Philosophical Library, 1968. 130 pp. Bibliographical footnotes.

Samuel, Arthur R. *Law as a Factor of Social Change: The Socio-Legal Philosophy of Louis Dembitz Brandeis.* Master of Arts diss. in the Department of Sociology. Louisville, Ky.: University of Louisville, 1963. 82 pp., typescript. Bibliography, pp. 80–82.

Samuel states that Brandeis used his socio-legal philosophy as a foundation for legal reform and social change.

Soviv, Aaron. *Louis D. Brandeis: The Champion for Justice.* (Zionist Personalities Series). New York: Jewish National Fund, Youth and Education Department, 1969. 32 pp., softcover.

Besides the text, the work contains many black and white photographs of Brandeis taken at different stages in his life.

Spelling, Thomas Crisp. *In Re Nomination of Louis D. Brandeis for Associate Justice, Supreme Court of the United States Now Pending in the United States Senate. Summary of Charges and Evidence.* New York, 1916. 96 pp., cover-title.

Stern, Ellen Norman. *Embattled Justice: The Story of Louis Dembitz Brandeis.* Philadelphia: Jewish Publications Society of America, 1971. 143 pp. Bibliography, p. 143.

It is a basic biography, written for young people.

Strum, Philippa. *Louis D. Brandeis: Justice for the People.* Cambridge, Mass.: Harvard University Press, 1984. 508 pp. Notes, pp. 421–485; bibliography, pp. 486–491; interviews (7), p. 486.

Professor Strum reveals new dimensions in Brandeis' life and his lifelong crusade for a better America.

Supreme Court of the United States. *Proceedings in Memory of Mr. Justice Brandeis.* 317 United States Reports ix-xlix (1942). [Listed by Mersky, on p. 30, under "U.S."] Reprinted in Jacobs, Roger F., comp. *Memorials of the Justices of the Supreme Court of the United States.* 4 vols. Littleton, Colo.: Fred B. Rothman & Co., 1981. Reprinted at pp. 159-214 of volume 1.

Theodor Herzl Institute. *In Recall of Greatness Upon the Twenty-Fifth Anniversary of the Passing of Louis D. Brandeis. Program Planning Guide and Kit.* New York, 1966. Various paginations, mimeographed.

> This is a series of non-scholarly papers and documents published to help people remember the event and honor Brandeis.
>
> Especially interesting is Tovia Preschel's *"An Imaginary Interview with Louis D. Brandeis on Issues of Our Times"* (8 pp.). Brandeis' words are based on his statements either given orally or in writing.

Todd, A. L. *Justice on Trial: The Case of Louis D. Brandeis.* New York: McGraw-Hill Book Company, 1964. 275 pp. Bibliography, pp. 263–267.

> The work is an historical survey of the bitter struggle over Brandeis' confirmation to the Supreme Court by the United States Senate in 1916, successfully fought by Wilson, Brandeis and their supporters.

Urofsky, Melvin I. *The Liberalism of Mr. Justice Brandeis.* Louisville, Ky.: University of Louisville School of Law, 1978. 18 pp., typescript.

> The work prints Professor Urofsky's speech which was delivered as the H. G. Handmaker Memorial Lecture, University of Louisville School of Law, on March 27, 1978.

———, *Louis D. Brandeis and the Progressive Tradition.* Boston: Little, Brown and Company, 1981. 183 pp. Bibliography, pp. 172–175.

> Urofsky narrates Brandeis' place in the American reform movement and social change.

———, *A Mind of One Piece: Brandeis and American Reform.* New York: Charles Scribner's Sons, 1971. 210 pp. Notes, pp. 171–200; bibliographical essay, pp. 201–205.

> Various aspects of Brandeis' life are explored by Urofsky. He documents Brandeis' position as a leading figure in the American reform movement.

Zionist Organization of America. *Program Guide and Sourcebook for the Brandeis Centennial Year.* New York, 1958. 20 pp.

> The work was produced to aid groups celebrate the 100th anniversary of Brandeis' birth. It contains basic information on him.

CHAPTER 2

Law Review and Legal Periodical Articles

Abrams, Floyd. "Brandeis After the 'Secret Connection.'" *New York Law Journal* 188(6): 2-3 (July 9, 1982).

Abrams agrees to a degree with Professor Murphy, but rejects as "unfair and unjust" Murphy's total treatment of Brandeis.

Acheson, Dean. "Recollections of Service with the Federal Supreme Court." *Alabama Lawyer* 18:355-366 (1957).

This is a reprint of a speech given by Dean Acheson to the American Law Institute on May 25, 1956 in Washington, D.C. It is an informal discussion of the United States Supreme Court and Justice Brandeis. Most of the address appears in Acheson's book, *Morning and Noon* (1965).

Andreola, Kathy. Book review: "The Brandeis/Frankfurter Connection." *Santa Clara Law Review* 23:703-709 (1983).

A critical appraisal of Professor Murphy's biography.

Annes, Paul G. "Brandeis—An Appreciation." *Decalogue Journal* 6(5): 15 (June-July 1956).

A one-page glowing tribute to the Justice.

Austern, H. Thomas. "The Parentage and Administrative Ontogeny of the Federal Trade Commission." *Antitrust Law Symposium* 1955:83-95.

Brandeis is briefly mentioned throughout the work. This is an address given by a former law clerk of Brandeis (1930-1931) to the Section on Antitrust Law of the New York State Bar Association on January 25, 1955. The meeting commemorates the fortieth anniversary of the creation of the Federal Trade Commission. Brandeis played a significant role in the creation of the agency.

Bagan. See under Notes.

Balman, Steven K. Book review: "The Brandeis/Frankfurter Connection." *Tulsa Law Review* 17:811–822 (1982).

The review discusses both the good and bad features of Professor Murphy's biography.

Barron, James H. "Warren and Brandeis, 'The Right to Privacy,' 4 Harv. L. Rev. 193 (1890): Demystifying a Landmark Citation." *Suffolk University Law Review* 13:875–922 (1979).

This article refutes the popular legend that Warren and Brandeis wrote their epic article as a response to great newspaper publicity regarding the forthcoming marriage of Warren's daughter. (See Prosser, "Privacy." *California Law Review* 48:383 (1960)) Barron states that she was only seven years old in 1890 (p. 893). The article also examines the Boston press of that era and the doctrine of privacy.

Bernard, Burton C. "Brandeis in St. Louis." *St. Louis Bar Journal* 11:53–68 (1964).

Bernard investigated the local records to analyze Brandeis' St. Louis law practice (1878–1879). Footnotes, pp. 62–68.

———, "Brandeis in Saint Louis." *St. Louis University Law Journal* 11:9–11 (1966).

This is the third part of a four-part speech tribute to Brandeis.

Betten, Alan. Book review: "The Brandeis/Frankfurter Connection." *University of Baltimore Law Review* 12:386–394 (1983).

A balanced review of Murphy's biography.

Blaustein, Albert P., and Roy M. Mersky. "Rating Supreme Court Justices." *American Bar Association Journal* 58:1183–1189 (1972).

The authors polled sixty-five law school deans and professors of law, of history and of political science as to who were the great United States Supreme Court justices. Brandeis received sixty-two votes and is ranked as a "great" justice.

Bloustein, Edward J. "Privacy, Tort Law, and the Constitution: Is Warren and Brandeis' Tort Petty and Unconstitutional as Well?" *Texas Law Review* 46:611–629 (1968).

Bloustein uses the Warren and Brandeis article as a starting point to discuss Professor Harry Kalven's article, "Privacy in Tort Law—Were Warren and Brandeis Wrong?" 31 *Law and Contemporary Problems* 326–341 (1966) and the then recent Supreme Court decisions on privacy.

Brenner, Saul. "Is Competence Related to Majority Opinion Assignment on the United States Supreme Court?" *Capital University Law Review* 15:35-41 (1985).

While Brandeis is usually placed in the "great" justices category, he received an extremely low score (1.4) on Professor Brenner's opinion assignment rations index. According to Brenner this is a striking exception to the general rule that "great" justices wrote the majority opinion in "great" cases. "Apparently, Brandeis was a man ahead of his time," at p. 39.

Brickner, Paul. Bibliographic essay: "Prophets of Regulation: . . . [and] Louis D. Brandeis: Justice for the People. . . ." *University of Cincinnati Law Review* 54:839-856 (1986).

Administrative Law Judge Brickner reviews in depth two recent books (by McCraw and Strum) on Brandeis. He likes both and concludes, "Both books are well written, interesting, and deserving of merit on the Brandeisian bookshelf," at p. 856.

————, Book review: "Brandeis. By Lewis J. Paper . . . [and] Louis D. Brandeis and the Progressive Tradition. By Melvin I. Urofsky. . . ." *Vanderbilt Law Review* 37:1041-1049 (1984).

This is a favorable review of two recent "popular" biographies of Brandeis.

————, Book review: "Brandeis and Frankfurter: A Dual Biography. By Leonard Baker." *Notre Dame Law Review* 60:621-627 (1985).

While a favorable book review, Brickner points out several flaws in the volume.

Bright, Myron H., in collaboration with David T. Smorodin. Book review: "A Flawed Tale: The Brandeis/Frankfurter Connection." *Loyola of Los Angeles Law Review* 16:205-226 (1983).

This is a highly critical review. He concludes, "Unfortunately, Murphy's book is neither a fair appraisal of their virtues nor of their faults," at p. 226.

Bryden, David P. "Brandeis's [sic] Facts." *Constitutional Commentary* 1:281-326 (1984).

Bryden discusses the famous Brandeis brief in *Muller v. Oregon* (208 U.S. 412 (1908)), his marshalling of facts, and labor conditions in the nineteenth century and the early part of the twentieth century.

————, "But cf . . . ." *Constitutional Commentary* 1:183-189 (1984).

The author recounts the treatment of Justices Brandeis and Holmes by law review authors in the 1920s.

Christensen, George A. "Here Lies the Supreme Court: Gravesites of the Justices." *Supreme Court Historical Society Yearbook* 1983:16–30.

The author tells where all the dead justices of the Supreme Court are buried. There is a paragraph on Brandeis' gravesite at the University of Louisville School of Law, at p. 20. In addition, there is a joint photograph of Mr. and Mrs. Brandeis, which was taken on his eighty-third birthday in 1939, also on p. 20.

Collins, Ronald K. L., and Jennifer Friesen. "Looking Back on Muller v. Oregon." *American Bar Association Journal* 69:294–298 (1983).

This is the first of a two-part article on this landmark decision, 208 U.S. 412 (1908). The second article, at p. 472, has Friesen as the first-listed author. The authors discuss Brandeis' role and his brief in this case and in later National Consumers' League cases.

Comments: "Mr. Justice Brandeis, Competition and Smallness: A Dilemma Re-Examined" (authored by Stephen A. Weiner). *Yale Law Journal* 66:69–96 (1956).

This analysis of Brandeis' economic thought was written to commemorate the 100th anniversary of his birth. [Listed by Mersky at p. 34, with Weiner as the author.]

Crowley, Michael L. Book review: "Brandeis, by Lewis J. Paper." *California Western Law Review* 20:539–542 (1984).

It is an extremely favorable review of Paper's biography of Brandeis. Crowley calls it readable, scholarly, informative, gossipy and well documented, at p. 539.

Currie, George R. "A Judicial All-Star Nine." *Wisconsin Law Review* 1964:3–31.

Currie selected Brandeis as a member of this elite team. Brandeis' tenure on the Supreme Court is discussed at pp. 23–27.

Dalton, Harlon L. Book review: "Off the Bench and Into the Mire: Judging Extrajudicial Behavior." *Yale Law Journal* 91:1708–1725 (1982).

It is an extremely critical review of Murphy's biography of Brandeis and Frankfurter.

Danelski, David J. Book review: "The Brandeis/Frankfurter Connection. . . ." *Harvard Law Review* 96:312–330 (1982).

This review is a partial defense and critique of Professor Murphy's book.

Denman, William. "Brandeis: His Advice to Young Men Seeking Public Careers—Religion in Politics." *California State Bar Journal* 11:306–311 (1936).

Federal Court of Appeals Judge Denman delivered this address as part of a commemoration of Justice Brandeis' eightieth birthday held in San Francisco in 1936. Denman relates his meetings with Brandeis over the years and quotes from many statements by Brandeis on life and public service.

Deutsch, J. G., and M. H. Hoeflich. "Legal Duty and Judicial Style: The Meaning of Precedent." *St. Louis University Law Journal* 25:87-96 (1981).

This article is an analysis of United States Senator Roman Hruska's statement when he defended President Nixon's nomination of G. Harold Carswell to the United States Supreme Court, "We can't have all Brandeises and Carodozos and Frankfurters . . . ," at p. 87, and how these three justices decided cases.

Dilliard, Irving, "Saint Louis Recalls Brandeis." *St. Louis University Law Journal* 11:12-14 (1966).

It is the fourth part of a four-speech tribute to the Justice.

Doro, Marion E. "The Brandeis Brief." *Vanderbilt Law Review* 11:783-799 (1958).

Doro discusses and dissects, in general, the philosophy of the Brandeis brief (which is defined in *Black's Law Dictionary*, 5th ed., (West Publishing Company, 1981, at p. 170) as a "[f]orm of appellate brief in which economic and social surveys and studies are included along with legal principles and citations and which takes its name from Louis D. Brandeis, former Associate Justice of Supreme Court, who used such brief while practicing law," and specifically, its use in the *Muller v. Oregon, New State Ice,* 285 U.S. 262, 280 (1932) cases and its application by later attorneys.

Dorsey, Gray L. "Brandeis Brief as Jurisprudence Source Material." *Law Library Journal* 51:16-20 (1958).

Dorsey discusses Brandeis' brief in *Muller v. Oregon,* 208 U.S. 412 (1908). In addition, Dorsey lists the briefs Brandeis wrote for the National Consumers' League.

Drubkin, Jess Howard. Book review: "The Brandeis/Frankfurter Connection. . . ." *Harvard Journal of Legislation* 19:443-447 (1982).

Drubkin wrote a balanced review of Professor Murphy's biography.

Ehrenhaft, Peter D. Book review: "Bruce Allen Murphy, The Brandeis/Frankfurter Connection. . . ." *American Journal of Legal History* 27:302-307 (1983).

The reviewer was "Senior law clerk to Chief Justice Earl Warren during Justice Frankfurter's last active term." In his review, Ehrenhaft probes the question if being a Supreme Court justice requires "total abstinence from the political life of the country," at p. 307.

Ferman, Irving. Book review: "Bruce Allen Murphy, The Brandeis/Frankfurter Connection. . . ." *Howard Law Journal* 26:345–358 (1983).

Ferman uses this book review as a starting point for a brief survey of Brandeis' career and his commitment to reform and justice. He concludes, "we must restrict the political activity of justices to open, non-partisan and mere expression of views," at p. 358.

Frank, John P. "The Legal Ethics of Louis D. Brandeis." *Stanford Law Review* 17:683–709 (1965).

Frank chronicles Brandeis' appointment to the United States Supreme Court in connection with his career as an attorney. His nomination by President Wilson unleashed a furious campaign of hate and slander against him. Frank discusses the charges made against Brandeis in 1916. The article is favorable to Brandeis. Frank concludes that Brandeis did "have a sense of the right, and confidence to act on it," at p. 709.

———, Review article: "Bruce Allen Murphy, The Brandeis/Frankfurter Connection. . . ." *Journal of Legal Education* 32:432–445 (1982).

It is a mostly favorable review of Murphy's book.

Frankfurter, Felix. "Mr. Justice Brandeis." Reprinted as "Justice Brandeis," in Hathaway, George H. "Plain English in Judicial Opinions." *Michigan Bar Journal* 62:976–978 (1983).

Frankfurter's article originally appeared in *Harvard Law Review* 55:181 (1941). It was chosen by Hathaway to illustrate good writing style. [The original article is on Mersky's list, at p. 31.]

Frantz, Laurent B. Book review: "The Brandeis/Frankfurter Connection. . . ." *The Guild Practitioner* 40:53–54 (1983).

This is a critical review.

French, John D. Book review: "The Brandeis/Frankfurter Connection." *Minnesota Law Review* 67:287–291 (1982).

It is a quite negative review of the Murphy book.

Freund, Paul A. "An Appreciation of Mr. Justice Brandeis." *St. Louis University Law Journal* 11:4–5 (1966).

Written by one of his former law clerks, it is the first part of a four-speech tribute to the Justice.

———, "Holmes and Brandeis in Retrospect." *Boston Bar Journal* 28(5): 7–10 (September/October 1984).

This article was adapted from a talk originally given by Professor Freund at a Speaker's Luncheon of the Boston Bar Association. The issue's cover is a 1927-28 photograph of Holmes and Brandeis standing together outside a building.

————, "The Supreme Court: A Tale of Two Terms." *Ohio State Law Journal* 26:225-238 (1965).

Freund relates a few of his experiences as Brandeis' law clerk and compares some of the cases decided in the October 1932 term with those of the October 1963 term. The article was given as the Walter J. Shepard Memorial Lecture at the Ohio State University College of Law on October 19, 1964.

Friendly, Henry J. "In Praise of *Erie*—and of the New Federal Common Law." *New York University Law Review* 39:383-422 (1964).

It is a defense of Brandeis' opinion in *Erie Railroad Co. v. Tompkins*, 304 U.S. 64 (1938). Judge Friendly, who was Brandeis' law clerk during the October 1927 term, argues that "... Mr. Justice Brandeis not only reached the right result but reached it for the only right reason . . . ," at p. 384. This article was reproduced in Friendly's book *Benchmarks*, see chap. 3, "Partials of Books," *infra.*

————, "Mr. Justice Brandeis: The Quest For Reason." *University of Pennsylvania Law Review* 108:985-999 (1960).

This article prints Judge Friendly's address that he delivered at the annual meeting of the Mississippi Valley Historical Association on April 29, 1960 in Louisville, Kentucky. This article was reprinted in Friendly's book *Benchmarks* (1967), see chap. 3, "Partials of Books," *infra.*

Friesen, Jennifer, and Ronald K. L. Collins. "Looking Back on Muller v. Oregon." *American Bar Association Journal* 69:472-477 (1983).

This is the second of a two-part article on this landmark decision, 208 U.S. 412 (1908). The first article has Collins as the first-listed author, at p. 294. The authors discuss Brandeis' role and his brief in this case and in later National Consumers' League cases.

Galloway, Russell W., Jr. "The Court That Challenged the New Deal (1930-1936)." *Santa Clara Law Review* 24:65-109 (1984).

The article analyzes the voting patterns of the Supreme Court justices from the October 1929 term through the October 1935 term. Galloway places Brandeis into the liberal bloc. During this time period, Brandeis dissented in 71 cases out of a possible 1,071 cases (6.6%), Table 25, at p. 90. The article contains a vast number of tables of statistics. The text discusses the tables.

————, "The Roosevelt Court: The Liberals Conquer (1937-1941) and Divide (1941-1946)." *Santa Clara Law Review* 23:491-542 (1983).

The voting patterns of the justices from the October 1936 term to the October 1945 term are discussed. Brandeis sat until February 13, 1939. The article is composed of both text and tables which divide the justices into liberal and conservative camps. Galloway ranks Brandeis as a liberal throughout his term on the High Court.

————, "The Taft Court (1921-29)." *Santa Clara Law Review* 25:1-64 (1985).

Professor Galloway explores the conservative Supreme Court during the time period October 1921 through October 1929. Former President William Howard Taft was the Chief Justice. During this era, Brandeis dissented in 91 cases out of 1,682, or 5.4%. The article also has numerous tables of statistics to show how the justices voted. Galloway puts Brandeis to the left of center.

Giekel, Jeffrey. "The Frankfurter Retainer—Ethical Implications for Bar." *New York Law Journal* 187(56): 1-2 (March 24, 1982).

It is a short discussion of the ethics of the Frankfurter-Brandeis financial arrangement.

Hambleton, James E. "The All-Time, All-Star, All-Era Supreme Court." *American Bar Association Journal* 69:462-464 (1983).

This short article reviews four lists of great judges. Brandeis is on two of them. Hambleton selects him for the "Team."

Handler, Janice. Book review: "Brandeis/Frankfurter Connection. . . ." *New York Law Journal* 187(53): 2 (March 19, 1982).

It is a critical review of the Murphy book.

Handler, Milton. "Introductory—The Brandeis Conception of the Relationship of Small Business to Antitrust." *A.B.A. Section of Antitrust Law, Proceedings of the Spring Meeting* 16:13-17 (April 1960).

————, "The Judicial Architects of The Rule of Reason." *A.B.A. Section of Antitrust Law, Proceedings of the Spring Meeting* 10:21-39 (April 1957).

Brandeis is discussed in this article at pp. 31-34.

Hart, Henry M., Jr. Book review: "Brandeis: Lawyer and Judge in the Modern State, by Alpheus Thomas Mason." *University of Pennsylvania Law Review* 82:668-670 (1934).

Written by a former law clerk of Brandeis, it is a critical and somewhat negative review.

Hathaway. See under Frankfurter.

Herbold, Sarah. Book review: "Brandeis, Frankfurter Political Alliance Probed. The Brandeis/Frankfurter Connection. . . ." *California Lawyer* 2(8): 91 (September 1982).

Although basically a straightforward review of the Murphy biography, Ms. Herbold is somewhat critical of his work.

Hofstadter, Samuel H. In Memoriam: "Louis Dembitz Brandeis." *American Bar Association Journal* 47:978-980 (1961).

This is a very favorable article that details Brandeis' jurisprudential philosophy. It was written to mark the twentieth anniversary of Brandeis' death.

———, "Mr. Justice Brandeis—Prophet In His Time." *New York Law Journal* 145(92): 4 (November 13, 1961); 145(93): 4 (November 14, 1961); 145(94): 4 (November 15, 1961).

Hufstedler, Shirley M. "Remembering Justice Louis D. Brandeis." *Journal of Family Law* 21:2-7 (1982).

Contains her remarks which were given before the Brandeis Society of the University of Louisville School of Law on May 6, 1982.

Jaffe, Louis L. "Was Brandeis an Activist? The Search for Intermediate Premises." *Harvard Law Review* 80:986-1003 (1967).

This essay was developed from Professor Jaffe's address given in 1966 at the University of Louisville honoring the fiftieth anniversary of the appointment to the Supreme Court of Mr. Justice Brandeis. He uses Dean Acheson's definition of activist (not a totally positive concept) and says Brandeis was above it. He concludes by saying of Brandeis, "He was a great judicial statesman," at p. 1003.

Jones, Gareth. Book review: "The Brandeis/Frankfurter Connection. . . ." *Cambridge Law Journal* 42:151-152 (1983).

It is a short book review of the Murphy biography.

Kalven, Harry, Jr. "Privacy in Tort Law—Were Warren and Brandeis Wrong?" *Law and Contemporary Problems* 31:326-341 (1966).

Kalven says "Warren and Brandeis were concerned only with public disclosure in the press of truthful but private details about the individual which caused emotional upset to him," at p. 330. But the concept of privacy has grown to take over the common law torts of libel and slander, at p. 341.

Kassan, Shalom. "Louis Dembitz Brandeis (1856-1941)—In Memoriam. (On' the 30th Anniversary of His Death.)" *Israel Law Review* 6:447-466 (1971).

It is an extremely favorable retelling of Brandeis' career, philosophy and tenure on the Supreme Court. Kassan concludes, "The spiritual and intellectual quality of this great man will be long valued and remembered," at p. 466.

Konefsky, Samuel J. Book review: "A Fresh Glimpse of Brandeis." *Virginia Law Review* 44:1093–1097 (1958).

This article reviews A. Bickel's book, *The Unpublished Opinions of Mr. Justice Brandeis* (1957), and Brandeis' role on the Supreme Court.

———, "Holmes and Brandeis: Companions in Dissent." *Vanderbilt Law Review* 10:269–300 (1957).

This is a reprint of chapter 6 and part of chapter 7 of Konefsky's biography *The Legacy of Holmes and Brandeis* (1956).

Kornstein, Daniel. "Brandeis—A Hero With Some Flaws." *New York Law Journal* 188(5): 2 (July 8, 1982).

The author refutes some of the arguments made by Professor Robert Cover in his *New Republic* article (listed in chap. 5, *infra*) that attacks the Murphy book.

———, "Brandeis's [*sic*] Changing Reputation." *New York Law Journal* 187(108): 2 (June 7, 1982).

This is a short and critical look at Brandeis. The article is based on Kornstein's reading the Murphy book and Hirsch's biography of Frankfurter.

Kronstein, Heinrich, and Joachim Volhard. "Brandeis Before the FTC in 1915: Should Advisory Opinions Be Given?" *Federal Bar Journal* 24:609–621 (1964).

The authors used the Federal Trade Commission files, which are stored in the National Archives, to write this article. They quote extensively from the files. Brandeis was one of the leaders in the movement to create this agency.

Kurland, Philip B. Book review: "Brandeis/Frankfurter Sensationalizes Serious Issue." *Legal Times of Washington* 4(44): 10, 13 (April 12, 1982).

It is a balanced review of the Murphy biography.

Levy, David W. "The Lawyer as Judge: Brandeis' View of the Legal Profession." *Oklahoma Law Review* 22:374–395 (1969).

It is in favorable view of the Justice as a practicing lawyer. Levy concludes it was "a profession which he loved, but which, he sometimes felt, failed to perform its most noble, promising, and important duties," at p. 395.

Levy, David W., and Bruce Allen Murphy. "Preserving the Progressive Spirit in A Conservative Time: The Joint Reform Efforts of Justice Brandeis and Professor Frankfurter, 1916–1933." *Michigan Law Review* 78:1252–1304 (1980).

Professors Levy and Murphy discuss the Brandeis/Frankfurter connection, Zionism and several other topics.

Lewis, Karen J., and Meridith McCoy. Book review: "A Tale of Two Justices: Not Yet Ready For Prime Time." *Federal Bar News and Journal* 29:359–360 (1982).

It is a critical book review of Murphy's biography.

Luban, David. Book review: "The Twice-Told Tale of Mr. Fixit: Reflections on the Brandeis/Frankfurter Connection." *Yale Law Journal* 91:1678–1707 (1982).

This is another critical review of the Murphy book.

McKay, Robert. Book review: "Revelations of a Smoke-Filled Courtroom." *Judicature* 66:163–165 (1982).

This is a favorable book review of the Murphy biography. McKay writes, Murphy "has written a remarkable book of demythology," at p. 163.

Marcus, Maeva. Book review: "Falling Under the Brandeis Spell. . . ." *Yale Law Journal* 95:195–206 (1985).

Professor Marcus specifically reviews the Baker and Strum biographies of Brandeis and, generally, the recent literature on the Justice. The review concludes that there still is "a need for systematic analysis of Brandeis' judicial contributions. . . . More should and will be done. And then, perhaps, we shall have all the information we need to assess, finally, the contributions of Louis D. Brandeis," at pp. 205–206.

Mason, Alpheus Thomas. "Louis Dembitz Brandeis: Tempered Boldness in a Stand-Pat Society." *University of Pittsburgh Law Review* 28:421–441 (1967).

It is a brief, favorable biography of Brandeis. This article was reprinted in L. Friedman and F. Israel's *The Justices of the United States Supreme Court 1789–1969: Their Lives and Major Opinions* (1969), vol. 3, pp. 2060–2073. Mason delivered this article originally as a speech at the Hebrew University Law School on December 6, 1966.

Mendelson, Wallace. "The Influence of James B. Thayer Upon the Work of Holmes, Brandeis and Frankfurter." *Vanderbilt Law Review* 31:71–87 (1978).

Brandeis studied constitutional law under Thayer at Harvard Law School. Later, they became personal friends. Thayer's concept of judicial restraint was "an act of the legislature is not to be declared void unless the violation of the Constitution is so manifest as to leave no room for reasonable doubt," at p. 73. Brandeis followed Thayer's doctrine of judicial restraint.

Miller, Authur S. Book review: "The Brandeis/Frankfurter Connection. . . ." *Nova Law Journal* 6:679–682 (1982).

Professor Miller wrote an extremely favorable review of Murphy's biography. Miller concludes, "If its minor errors are corrected in a subsequent printing, it deserves serious consideration for a Pulitzer Prize or National Book Award," at p. 682.

Murphy, Bruce Allen. "Elements of Extrajudicial Strategy: A Look at the Political Roles of Justices Brandeis and Frankfurter." *Georgetown Law Journal* 69:101–132 (1980).

This article was originally a speech given by Murphy in 1978, and later incorporated into his biography of Brandeis and Frankfurter.

Murphy, Paul L. "The Recent Fascination with Louis D. Brandeis." *Wisconsin Law Review* 1984:1391–1400.

Murphy discusses Baker's joint biography of Brandeis and Frankfurter and Professor Strum's biography of Brandeis. Both were published in 1984. He praises highly the Strum work, at p. 1400.

Nathanson, Nathaniel L. Book review: "Lewis J. Paper, Brandeis." *Journal of Legal Education* 34:142–143 (1984).

While Nathanson believes Paper succeeded in writing a biography of Brandeis that humanizes him, concludes his review that "there is still room for another book seriously addressed to the question why was Brandeis 'one of America's truly great Supreme Court justices,'" at p. 143.

———, Book review: "The Extra-Judicial Activities of Supreme Court Justices: Where Should the Line be Drawn? An Inquiry Stimulated by the Brandeis/Frankfurter Connection. . . ." *Northwestern University Law Review* 78:494–525 (1983).

It is a vigorous defense of Justices Brandeis and Frankfurter, written by one of Brandeis' former law clerks.

———, "The Philosophy of Mr. Justice Brandeis and Civil Liberties Today." *University of Illinois Law Forum* 1979: 261–300.

Professor Nathanson's remarks were originally delivered at the University of Illinois College of Law on November 16, 1978 as the first lecture of the David C. Baum Lectures on Civil Rights and Civil Liberties. It was reprinted in the book *Six Justices on Civil Rights*, edited by Ronald D.

Rotunda, Oceana Publications, (1983). Nathanson concludes, "Would that we could all follow in his footsteps," at p. 300.

Notes: "Louis Dembitz Brandeis—"Of The People, By The People, For The People" (authored by Earl Stephen Bagan). *Oklahoma City University Law Review* 9:505-539 (1984).

This is an extremely favorable review of Justice Brandeis' career.

Notes: "The Right to Privacy in Nineteenth Century America." *Harvard Law Review* 94:1892-1910 (1981).

The article shows that the right to privacy existed to some degree before Warren and Brandeis wrote their celebrated article.

O'Connor, Sandra D. Remarks of: "Being the Swinford Lecture." *Kentucky Bench and Bar* 49(3): 20-22, 51-53 (Summer 1985).

Justice O'Connor discusses Brandeis as one of the eleven Kentuckians out of a total of 103 Justices who served on the Supreme Court. This is a high figure given the small population of the state.
   The speech was delivered as the biennial Judge Mac Swinford Lecture, jointly sponsored by the Kentucky Bar Association and the University of Kentucky College of Law on September 6, 1984, at the Law School.

Paper, Lewis J. "Brandeis: Finding the Private Man." *Boston Bar Journal* 28(1): 4-8 (January/February 1984).

Paper discusses why he wrote his biography of Brandeis and several contradictions in Brandeis' life. Paper gave this article as a speech at Brandeis University in 1983 as The Rolde Memorial Lecture.

———, "The Not So Sinister Brandeis-Frankfurter Connection." *American Bar Association Journal* 69:1860-1864 (1983).

The article is excerpted from Paper's biography of Justice Brandeis. It also contains several informal photographs of Brandeis.

Petty, Phillip. Book review: "The Brandeis/Frankfurter Connection." *Western State University Law Review* 10:229-231 (1983).

This review is favorable to Professor Murphy's book. Judge Petty concludes, "Bruce Murphy's book is an incisive and helpful tool for those whose goal is judicial improvement in our time," at p. 231.

Pratt, Walter F. "The Warren and Brandeis Argument For a Right to Privacy." *Public Law* 1975:161-179.

Written from the British perspective, the author uses English cases to claim that there was no legal precedent for the right of privacy.

Pritchett, C. Herman. Book review: "The Brandeis/Frankfurter Connection." *University of Pennsylvania Law Review* 130:1281–1288 (1982).

Is a quite negative review of the Murphy work.

Rabban, David M. "The Emergence of Modern First Amendment Doctrine." *University of Chicago Law Review* 50:1205–1355 (1983).

Brandeis is mentioned throughout, especially at pp. 1320–1345. Rabban focuses on Brandeis' dissent in the *Whitney* case, 274 U.S. 357, 372 (1927).

Radocha, D. J. "Brandeis Today." *Loyola Law Times* 2:18–20, 22 (Winter 1962).

A brief, very favorable sketch of Brandeis' career and philosophy.

Resnik, Judith. Book review: "The Brandeis/Frankfurter Connection. . . ." *California Law Review* 71:776–794 (1983).

This is a somewhat critical review of the Murphy book.

Rogat, Yosal, and James M. O'Fallon. "Mr. Justice Holmes: A Dissenting Opinion—The Speech Cases." *Stanford Law Review* 36:1349–1406 (1984).

The Holmes-Brandeis "partnership" is analyzed at pp. 1389–1394 under the heading, "With Brandeis in Dissent."

Rotenberg, Mark B. Book review: "Politics, Personality and Judging: The Lessons of Brandeis and Frankfurter on Judicial Restraint." *Columbia Law Review* 83:1863–1887 (1983).

Rotenberg reviews both the Murphy joint biography of Brandeis and Frankfurter and Hirsch's book, *Enigma of Felix Frankfurter* (1981) in this article. While Rotenberg criticizes Murphy's literary style, he sees the book as a valuable contribution to the ongoing discussion of the ethical problems involved when judges participate in extrajudicial activities.

Sargent, Francis W. "Louis D. Brandeis: The Idea of Federalism and the Concept of Responsibility—A Lesson For Our Times." *Massachusetts Law Quarterly* 54:187–201 (1969).

Sargent discusses Brandeis and the doctrine of federalism. The article was adapted from his Shluger Memorial Lecture, delivered at Brandeis University.

Schlesinger, Robert N. Book review: "Brandeis, by Lewis J. Paper." *Hamline Law Review* 7:543–550 (1984).

This is a fairly favorable review of the Paper book.

Shapiro, Fred R. "The Most-Cited Law Review Articles." *California Law Review* 73:1540–1554 (1985).

On his list of unquestioned "classic" pre-1947 law review articles, Shapiro ranks first Warren and Brandeis' "The Right to Privacy" article, at p. 1545.

It is interesting to note that of Shapiro's fifty most-cited post-1947 law review articles, six were written by Brandeis' law clerks. Henry J. Friendly wrote number 39. Henry M. Hart, Jr. wrote numbers 17, 22, and 27 (a tie with Frankfurter) and 30. Harry Shulman wrote number 36, at pp. 1550-1551.

Shenfield, Arthur. "The Influence of Holmes and Brandeis on Labor Law," *Government Union Review* 3(3): 30-54 (Summer 1982).

It is an extremely positive view of these two Justices.

Shulman, Harry. Book review: "Brandeis: The Personal History of an American Ideal. By Alfred Lief." *Yale Law Journal* 46:724-727 (1937).

It is a book review written by one of Brandeis' former law clerks. Shulman believed that a biography of Brandeis should be five volumes in length, at p. 725. So far, all biographies have been only one volume in length.

Simon, William H. "Babbitt v. Brandeis: The Decline of the Professional Ideal." *Stanford Law Review* 37:565-587 (1985).

This article was written as part of a Symposium on the Corporate Law Firm held at Stanford Law School. "Babbitt" is Sinclair Lewis' protagonist. Simon ranks Brandeis as one of the two most influential expositors of the Progressive-Functionist vision, at p. 565.

Smurl, James F. "Allocating Public Burdens: The Social Ethics Implied in Brandeis of Boston." *Journal of Law and Religion* 1:59-78 (1983).

Analyzes Brandeis' social ethics in the context of his successful battle in 1893 against the West End Railway's (a Boston elevated company) efforts to obtain a franchise extending its trolley tracks across the Boston Common. Brandeis called this struggle his "first important public work," at p. 62.

Stark, Steven. "The Real Meaning of *Erie*." *Connecticut Law Review* 17:723-728 (1985).

The *Erie* decision (304 U.S. 64 (1938)) is one of Brandeis' most enduring contributions to American legal jurisprudence. The opinion has a life of its own.

Stark discusses *Erie* on philosophical grounds as a symbol, for he believes "Lawyers have cases for heroes," at p. 724. For Stark, *Erie* explains how the game is played. But he concludes the article with these words, "The real meaning of *Erie* is, alas, that it has no meaning at all," at p. 728.

Steinberg, Michael W. Book review: "Brandeis, Frankfurter and Judicial Conduct." *American Bar Association Journal,* 68:716-717 (1982).

This is a balanced book review of the Murphy biography.

Steiner, E. E. "A Progressive Creed: The Experimental Federalism of Justice Brandeis." *Yale Law & Policy Review* 2:1–48 (1983).

Steiner uses Brandeis' dissent in the *New State Ice Co.* case (285 U.S. 262, 280 (1932)) as a starting point to show Brandeis' concern for the doctrine of experimental federalism.

"A Tribute to Mr. Justice Brandeis." *St. Louis University Law Journal* 11:2–14 (1966).

This is a four-speech tribute to Brandeis given on June 28, 1966 at the Old Courthouse in St. Louis by Bernard, Dilliard, Freund and Whittaker to commemorate the fiftieth anniversary of his appointment to the United States Supreme Court. Each speech is listed in this chapter.

Urofsky, Melvin I. "The Brandeis-Frankfurter Conversations." *Supreme Court Review* 1985:299–339.

Professor Urofsky located, in the Brandeis Papers at the Harvard Law Library, notes made by Felix Frankfurter of his and Brandeis' conversations, held during the summers of 1922 to 1939, but mostly 1922 to 1924, at Brandeis' summer home at Chatham, Massachusetts.
   Urofsky has transcribed Frankfurter's notes, although some words remain impossible to read. Also, Urofsky annotated the transcripts by explaining the cases and people referred to.

———, "Louis D. Brandeis on Legal Education," *American Journal of Legal History* 22:189–201 (1978).

Urofsky describes Brandeis' philosophy of legal education and his role in the development of the University of Louisville School of Law Library and Harvard Law School.

———, "Myth and Reality: The Supreme Court and Protective Legislation in the Progressive Era." *Supreme Court Historical Society Yearbook* 1983:53–72.

Brandeis is mentioned briefly in this article. It includes a photograph of a youthful looking middle-age Brandeis, on p. 53.

———, "The 'Outrageous' Brandeis Nomination." *Supreme Court Historical Society Yearbook* 1979:8–19.

This is a retelling of the bitter confirmation process.

Vaughan, Frederick. Book review: "The Brandeis/Frankfurter Connection." *Supreme Court Law Review* 5:431–435 (1983).

This is a favorable review by a Canadian Professor of Political Studies. It is one of the few non-American reviews of the Murphy book.

Velvel, Lawrence R. Book review: "Brandeis/Frankfurter: Many Still Have Questions." *Legal Times of Washington* 4(50): 13, 14 (May 24, 1982).

This is a balanced review of the Murphy biography.

Weiner, Stephen A. See under Comments, this chapter.

Werner, Walter. "Corporation Law in Search of its Future." *Columbia Law Review* 81:1611–1666 (1981).

Werner discusses Brandeis', Willard Hurst's (a former Brandeis law clerk) and Adolf A. Berle's philosophy of corporation law.

Westin, Alan F. "Out-Of-Court Commentary by United States Supreme Court Justices, 1790–1962: Of Free Speech and Judicial Lockjaw." *Columbia Law Review* 62:633–669 (1962).

While Brandeis is mentioned only in passing, Westin makes this informative statement, "From the day he became a Justice in 1916, for example, Louis D. Brandeis said nothing in public about Court matters," at p. 635.

Wheeler, Russell R. Book review: "Of Standards for Extra-Judicial Behavior. The Brandeis/Frankfurter Connection." *Michigan Law Review* 81:931–945 (1983).

This is a positive review of Professor Murphy's book.

White, G. Edward. "Allocating Power Between Agencies and Courts: The Legacy of Justice Brandeis." *Duke Law Journal* 1974:195–244. Reprinted in *I.C.C. Practitioners Journal* 43:79–122 (1975).

The article reviews the history of administrative agencies, judicial courts, Brandeis' philosophy (which White calls "pragmatic theory"), and Brandeis' role in the development of American administrative law.

Whittaker, Charles Evans. "Reflections on Mr. Justice Brandeis." *St. Louis University Law Journal* 11:6–8 (1966).

It is the second part of a four-speech tribute to Brandeis. Whittaker was an Associate Justice of the Supreme Court from 1957 to 1962.

Wise, Edward M. Book review: "Brandeis by Lewis J. Paper." *Wayne Law Review* 30:183–189 (1983).

This is a critical review of Lewis' biography. Wise concludes, "Brandeis deserves better," at p. 189.

Woldman, Albert A. "Justice Louis D. Brandeis: Crusader for Human Rights." *Cleveland Bar Association Journal* 28:67, 72–80 (1957).

It is an extremely favorable biographical sketch of Brandeis.

Zimmerman, Diane L. "Requiem For a Heavyweight: A Farewell to Warren and Brandeis's Privacy Tort." *Cornell Law Review* 68:291–367 (1983).

Professor Zimmerman examines the Warren-Brandeis Privacy article in the context of modern American life which she calls "information-obsessed," at p. 364. Her thesis is that the concept of privacy (the right to be let alone) does not work and should be abandoned.

CHAPTER 3

Partials of Books: Justice Brandeis is Discussed at Some Length in These Works, But He is Not the Main Subject

Abraham, Henry J. *Justices and Presidents: A Political History of Appointments to the Supreme Court.* 2d ed. New York: Oxford University Press, 1985. 430 pp.

Brandeis is mentioned often throughout both editions, the first is copyrighted 1974, 310 pages. His confirmation struggle, which lasted four months, is described at pp. 178-181. The final Senate vote was 47 for, 22 against, and 27 not voting.

Acheson, Dean. *Morning and Noon.* Boston: Houghton Mifflin Company, 1965. 288 pp.

Chapters 3, 4, and 5 (pp. 40-103) are the finest description I have read of the duties of being Brandeis' law clerk. Acheson served two one-year terms as Brandeis' law clerk. He comments also on the various justices he met during his clerkship, 1919-1921.

Alofsin, Dorothy. "To the Rescue: Louis D. Brandeis." In *America's Triumph: Stories of American Jewish Heroes,* 136-163. New York: Union of American Hebrew Congregations, 1949. 312 pp.

This is a quite basic treatment of Brandeis' life and career.

Asch, Sidney H. "Louis D. Brandeis—Social Reformer with a Balance Sheet." Chap. 7 in *The Supreme Court and Its Great Justices,* 103-116. New York: Arco Publishing Co., 1971. 266 pp.

It is a condensed telling of Brandeis' life and Brandeis' role as a reformer in economic, legal and social areas. In addition, Brandeis is mentioned in other portions of the book in conjunction with other justices.

Baker, Liva. *Felix Frankfurter.* New York: Coward-McCann, Inc., 1969. 376 pp.

The Brandeis-Frankfurter relationship is discussed throughout this biography.

Barbar, James. *The Honorable Eighty-Eight.* New York: Vantage Press, 1957. 124 pp.

A thumbnail sketch of Brandeis appears at pp. 92-93.

Barnard, Harry. *The Forging of an American Jew: The Life and Times of Judge Julian W. Mack.* New York: Herzl Press, 1974. 346 pp.

Mack was one of the leaders of the American Zionist movement during the first part of the twentieth century. As a federal judge, at different times, he hired Nathaniel Nathanson and Thomas Austern to be his law clerks. After a year with Mack, each man later became Brandeis' law clerk. Brandeis is mentioned throughout.

Barth, Alan. "The Right Most Valued By Civilized Men." Chap. 3 in *Prophets with Honor: Great Dissents and Great Dissenters in the Supreme Court,* 54-79. New York: Alfred A. Knopf, Inc., 1974. 254 pp.

The chapter discusses the *Olmstead* case (277 U.S. 438 (1928)), Brandeis' dissent, which begins on p. 471, and the concept of privacy. His dissent is mentioned in other portions of the book and is reprinted in full in Appendix B, pp. 207-217.

Berlin, William S. "Louis Brandeis: The Liberal as Jew." Chap. 2 in *On the Edge of Politics: The Roots of Jewish Political Thought in America,* 21-45. Westport, Conn.: Greenwood Press, 1978. 206 pp.

The chapter retells his life as a Jew. Brandeis is mentioned in other chapters in connection with the subject matter of the chapter.

Berlin, William Stephen. *The Roots of Jewish Political Thought in America.* Ph.D. diss. New Brunswick, N.J.: Rutgers University, 1976. 278 leaves.

Berlin's dissertation is the basis for his work *On the Edge of Politics,* listed above.

Berman, Hyman. *Era of the Protocol: A Chapter in the History of the International Ladies Garment Workers' Union, 1910-1916.* Ph.D. diss., New York: Columbia University, 1956. 467 pp.

Brandeis served as one of its arbitrators before becoming a Justice.

Bickel, Alexander M., and Benno C. Schmidt, Jr. *The Judiciary and Responsible Government, 1910-21.* History of the Supreme Court of the United States (The Oliver Wendell Holmes Devise), vol. 9. New York: Macmillan Publishing Company, 1984. 1041 pp.

Bickel describes the first years (1916–1921) of Brandeis' tenure on the high court.

Campbell, Tom Walter. "Louis D. Brandeis." Chap. 63 in *Four Score Forgotten Men: Sketches of the Justices of the U.S. Supreme Court*, 337–341. Little Rock, Ark.: Pioneer Publishing Company, 1950. 424 pp.

The article outlines his career on the high court.

Cohen, Morris Raphael. "Louis D. Brandeis." Chap. 2 in *The Faith of a Liberal: Selected Essays*, 32–39. New York: Henry Holt and Co., 1946. 497 pp.

This essay was published originally in *Harvard Law Review* 47:164 (1933) as Cohen's book review of Felix Frankfurter's *Mr. Justice Brandeis*.

Daly, John J. *The Use of History in the Decisions of the Supreme Court: 1900–1930*. Washington, D.C.: The Catholic University of America Press, 1954. 233 pp.

This book is Daly's Ph.D. dissertation in Philosophy. It is one of a series of studies done at the Catholic University of America on the use of historical data to support legal arguments in Supreme Court decisions.
Brandeis is quoted often and extensively referred to as a Justice who used history in his judicial opinions.

Dash, Joan. *Summoned to Jerusalem: The Life of Henrietta Szold*. New York: Harper & Row, Publishers, 1979. 348 pp.

Brandeis is mentioned often, especially at pp. 114–120 in connection with Mrs. Szold's Zionist efforts.

Davis, Mac. "Louis D. Brandeis: The First Judge for the Supreme Court." In *Jews at a Glance*, p. 28. New York: Hebrew Publishing Co., 1956. 127 pp.

This is, obviously, a brief treatment.

Douglas, William Orville. "Brandeis and Black." Chap. 25 in *Go East, Young Man: The Early Years. The Autobiography of William O. Douglas*, 441–453. New York: Random House, 1974. 493 pp.

It contains a thumbnail sketch of Brandeis (pp. 448–449) and Brandeis' general influence upon Douglas' judicial practices and ideas. Douglas replaced Brandeis on the Supreme Court in 1939.

Eiseman, Alberta. "Let Our Minds Be Bold." Chap. 3 in *Rebels and Reformers: Biographies of Four Jewish Americans*, 67–98. Garden City, N.Y.: Zenith Books, 1976. 131 pp.

The chapter recounts Brandeis' life in simple language. The other three biographies are of: Uriah Phillips Levy, Ernestine L. Rose, and Lillian D. Wald.

Ernst, Morris L. "The Case of People versus Property," and "A Day in Court for the Poor." Chaps. 8 and 9 in *The Great Reversals: Tales of the Supreme Court*, 100–118, 119–135. New York: Weybright and Talley, 1973. 212 pp.

This book was written for lay people, not lawyers. Ernst wrote in his foreword that "Judge Brandeis was one of the important mentors in my life." Brandeis gave him the lamp which was before him on the Supreme Court bench.

Ernst writes of Brandeis in two chapters in the realm of a social reformer, both before he joined the High Court as well as afterwards.

Feingold, Henry L. *A Midrash on American Jewish History*. Albany: State University of New York Press, 1982. 241 pp.

Feingold briefly traces the contribution of Brandeis in legitimizing Zionism as a respectable "American" idealogy.

Flynn, James J. "Louis David Brandeis." In *Famous Justices of the Supreme Court*, 101–108. New York: Dodd, Mead & Company, 1968. 157 pp.

Brandeis is discussed. This volume is written for juveniles.

Because of respect for his mother's brother, Lewis Dembitz, Brandeis changed his middle name from David to Dembitz. Brandeis went to law school and became an attorney because this uncle, Lewis Dembitz, was a prominent Louisville lawyer.

Fox, Maier B. *American Zionism in the 1920s*. Ph.D. diss. Washington, D.C.: George Washington University, 1979. 451 pp.

Frankfurter, Felix. *Felix Frankfurter Reminisces. Recorded in Talks with Dr. Harlan B. Phillips*. New York: Reynal & Company, 1960. 310 pp.

Brandeis is mentioned throughout this book.

————, *From the Diaries of Felix Frankfurter: With a Biographical Essay and Notes by Joseph P. Lash*. New York: W. W. Norton & Co. Inc., 1975. 366 pp.

Brandeis' name appears throughout.

————, "Louis Dembitz Brandeis." Chap. 8 in *Of Law and Life & Other Things That Matter. Papers and Addresses of Felix Frankfurter, 1956–1963*, edited by Philip B. Kurland, 54–62. Cambridge, Mass.: The Belknap Press of Harvard University Press, 1965. 257 pp.

This is a reprint of Frankfurter's November 11, 1956 *New York Times Magazine* article, "The Moral Grandeur of Justice Brandeis" [which is listed by Mersky, at p. 36].

Freund, Paul A. "Mr. Justice Brandeis." In *On Law and Justice*, 119–145. Cambridge, Mass.: The Belknap Press of Harvard University Press, 1968. 259 pp.

It is a reprint of his *Harvard Law Review* 70:769 (1957) essay on Brandeis.

————, "Portrait of a Liberal Judge: Mr. Justice Brandeis." Chap. 5 in *The Supreme Court of the United States: Its Business, Purposes and Performance*, 116–144. Cleveland, Meridian Books, World Publishing Co., 1961. 224 pp.

Besides discussing Brandeis in chapter 5, Freund, one of his former law clerks, criticizes the use of the "Brandeis brief" in post–World War II civil rights cases, at pp. 150–154. Freund used a large portion of his earlier work, *On Understanding the Supreme Court* (1949) in writing this monograph.

Freyer, Tony. *Harmony & Dissonance: The Swift and Erie Cases in American Federalism*. New York: New York University Press, 1981. 190 pp.

Brandeis wrote the majority opinion in *Erie Railroad Co. v. Tompkins*, 304 U.S. 64 (1938), which is discussed at pp. 101–164. Said decision reversed *Swift v. Tyson*, 41 U.S. (16 Peters) 1 (1842).

Friendly, Fred W. *Minnesota Rag: The Dramatic Story of the Landmark Supreme Court Case That Gave New Meaning to Freedom of the Press*. New York: Random House, 1981. 243 pp.

Brandeis' role in the *Near v. Minnesota* decision (283 U.S. 697 (1931)) is discussed throughout this book.

Friendly, Henry J. "In Praise of *Erie*—And of the New Federal Common Law" and "Mr. Justice Brandeis—The Quest for Reason." Chaps. 9 and 14 in *Benchmarks*, 155–195, 291–307. Chicago: University of Chicago Press, 1967. 324 pp.

Friendly was one of Brandeis' law clerks.

    The essay comprising chapter 9 was originally given as the twenty-first annual Benjamin N. Cardozo lecture, delivered before the Association of the Bar of the City of New York on January 16, 1964 and was printed in: *Record of the Association of the Bar of the City of New York* 19:64–109 (1964) and in the *New York University Law Review* 39:383–422 (1964). The address is a defense of the *Erie* decision and doctrine.

    Most of the essay comprising chapter 14 was published originally in the *University of Pennsylvania Law Review* 108:985–999 (1960).

Friesel, Evyatar, ed. *Julius Simon: Certain Days—Zionist Memoirs and Selected Papers*. Jerusalem: Israel Universities Press, 1971. 385 pp.

Simon (1875–1969) is a little known American Zionist leader, who was associated with Justice Brandeis in the Zionist movement. Simon tried but was unable to work out a compromise between Weizmann and Brandeis over the direction the American Zionist movement should follow.

Frommer, Morris. *The American Jewish Congress: A History, 1914-1950*. Ph.D. diss. Columbus: Ohio State University, 1978. 2 vols. (563 pp).

Gersh, Harry. "Louis D. Brandeis." In *These Are My People: A Treasury of Biographies of Heroes of the Jewish Spirit from Abraham to Leo Baeck*, 308-316. New York: Behrman House, Inc., 1959. 408 pp.

Gersh focuses on Brandeis' crusading efforts.

Girgus, Sam B. "The American Way: From the Colonial Era to Louis Brandeis, Sidney Hillman and the Liberal Consensus. Chap. 3 in *The New Covenant: Jewish Writers and the American Idea*, 37-63. Chapel Hill, University of North Carolina Press, 1984. 220 pp.

Girgus believes that three concepts merged in Brandeis' later years to form one consistent philosophy. The concepts are: one, the progressive and reformist theories; two, concern for the daily working lives and circumstances of the common man; and three, connection between Judaism and Americanism, at pp. 47-48.

Goldmark, Josephine Clara. "The Brandeis Brief." Chap. 13 in *Impatient Crusader: Florence Kelley's Life Story*, 143-159. Urbana: University of Illinois Press, 1953. 217 pp.

In addition to this chapter, he is mentioned often elsewhere. Kelley played a key role in the National Consumers' League. This biography was written by her younger co-worker in the movement.

Haber, Samuel. *Efficiency and Uplift: Scientific Management in the Progressive Era, 1890-1920*. Chicago: University of Chicago Press, 1964. 181 pp.

Haber describes Brandeis' role in the introduction of the concept of scientific management beginning with his testimony before the Interstate Commerce Commission in 1910 on the "Eastern Rate Case." Brandeis, who represented Eastern business associations who opposed the railroads proposed rate increase, argued for more efficiency in running the railroads. He brought to the Commission's hearings many witnesses to prove that the railroads could save $1,000,000 per day by scientific management.

Hagedorn, Hermann. "Louis Dembitz Brandeis." In *Americans: A Book of Lives*, 207-224. New York: The John Day Company, 1946. 392 pp.

Hand, Learned. "Mr. Justice Brandeis." In *The Spirit of Liberty: Papers and Addresses of Learned Hand, collected, and with an introduction and notes* by Irving Dilliard, 166-174. 3d ed., enl. New York: Alfred A. Knopf, Inc., 1960. 311 pp.

These pages reproduce federal Judge Hand's address given at the memorial service for Brandeis, which was held at the United States Supreme Court on December 21, 1942. The entire ceremony is reprinted in Supreme Court of the United States. *Proceedings . . .* (see chapter 1, *infra*).

Hawley, Ellis W. *The New Deal and the Problem of Monopoly: A Study in Economic Ambivalence.* Princeton, N.J.: Princeton University Press, 1966. 525 pp.

Brandeis and four of his former law clerks (Acheson, Freund, Landis and Magruder) who served in various New Deal agencies, are mentioned often.

Hirsch, H. N. *The Enigma of Felix Frankfurter.* New York: Basic Books, Inc., 1981. 253 pp.

While the author's primary focus is on Frankfurter, Brandeis is alluded to throughout the volume.

Irons, Peter H. *The New Deal Lawyers.* Princeton, N.J.: Princeton University Press, 1982. 351 pp.

Brandeis and the Supreme Court during the New Deal is discussed. The author concedes that he neglected Dean Acheson and James M. Landis (former Brandeis law clerks) and several others as they were primarily administrators, not litigators, at p. xii.

Jackson, Percival E. *Dissent in the Supreme Court: A Chronology.* Norman: University of Oklahoma Press, 1969. 583 pp.

Brandeis' dissents are discussed throughout.

Johnson, John W. "A Revolution in Legal Analysis: The Strategic Genius of Louis Brandeis." Chap. 3 in *American Legal Culture, 1908-1940,* 29-51. Westport, Conn.: Greenwood Press, 1981. 185 pp.

Johnson investigates Brandeis, the Brandeis brief and his use of non-legal sources of information in his Supreme Court opinions.

Karfunkel, Thomas, and Thomas W. Ryley. "Brandeis." Chap. 2 in *The Jewish Seat: Anti-Semitism and the Appointment of Jews to the Supreme Court.* 37-58. Hicksville, N.Y.: Exposition Press, 1978, 164 pp.

Knee, Stuart E. "House Divided: Brandeis Zionism Versus Weizmann Zionism." Chap. 5 in *The Concept of Zionist Dissent in the American Mind, 1917-1941,* 117-153. New York: Robert Speller & Sons, 1980. 268 pp.

This chapter recounts their struggle.

La Follette, Belle, and Fola La Follette. "Brandeis Becomes Our Friend." Chap. 26 in *Robert M. La Follette, June 14, 1885-June 18, 1925,* 286-291. New York: The Macmillan Company, 1953. 1305 pp. 2 vols.

The book reveals the close and lasting friendship between La Follette and Brandeis. They first met in Washington, D.C., in 1910. Brandeis is mentioned often beginning with chapter 26.

Levitan, Tina Nellie. "The First United States Supreme Court Justice." Biography no. 78 in *The Firsts of American Jewish History, 1492-1951,* 123-125. 1st ed. Brooklyn, N.Y.: The Charuth Press, 1952. 172 pp.

————, "The First Jewish Supreme Court Justice, 1916." In *The Firsts of American Jewish History, 1492-1956,* 192-195. 2d ed. Brooklyn, N.Y.: The Charuth Press, 1957. 285 pp.

This is a brief word portrait of Brandeis.

————, "1916: Louis D. Brandeis: First Jewish Supreme Court Justice." In *Jews in American Life,* 194-196. New York: Hebrew Publishing Co., 1969. 253 pp.

Lippmann, Walter. "Louis D. Brandeis." in *Public Persons,* 139-143. Edited by Gilbert A. Harrison. New York: Liveright Books, 1976. 189 pp.

The article is dated February 16, 1939, a few days after Brandeis resigned from the Supreme Court. Lippmann concludes this column with these words, "And because Louis D. Brandeis did so much more than any of his contemporaries to preserve the faith in the validity of that ideal, historians will call him, I think, the most influential American conservative of his age," at p. 142.

Lipsky, Louis. "Louis D. Brandeis (1856-1941)." In *A Gallery of Zionist Profiles,* 153-166. New York: Farrar, Straus & Cudahy, 1956. 226 pp.

This selection focuses on Brandeis' Zionist Activities. It was reprinted in his *Memoirs in Profile,* (1975) at pp. 201-211 (see below).

————, "Louis D. Brandeis (1856-1941)." In *Memoirs in Profile,* 201-211. Philadephia: Jewish Publications Society of America, 1975. 669 pp.

It reprints his article on Brandeis that appeared in his *A Gallery of Zionist Profiles* (listed above). Besides this chapter, Brandeis is mentioned extensively.

McCraw, Thomas K. "Brandeis and the Origins of the FTC." Chap. 3 in *Prophets of Regulation: Charles Francis Adams, Louis D. Brandeis, James M. Landis, Alfred E. Kahn,* 80-142. Cambridge, Mass.: The Belknap Press of Harvard University Press, 1984. 387 pp.

Professor McCraw illustrates many faults in Brandeis' theories of governmental regulation. The author rejects as wrong Brandeis' economic views. However, he credits Brandeis for deeply influencing the creation and evolution of governmental regulations. McCraw describes Brandeis' role in the development of administrative law in chapter 3. Landis was Brandeis' eighth law clerk.

McCraw, Thomas K., ed. "Testing a Prevalent Analysis: Louis D. Brandeis and the Antitrust Tradition." Part II of chap. 1 in *Regulation in Perspective: Historical Essays,* 25-55. Cambridge, Mass.: Division of Research, Graduate School of Business Administration, Harvard University, 1981. 246 pp.

Professor McCraw critically evaluates Brandeis' philosophy, which was against big business, for smallness and the "little guy."

McCune, Wesley. Pages 239-240 in *The Nine Young Men.* New York: Harper & Brothers, 1947. 299 pp.

Brandeis is briefly discussed.

Madison, Charles Allan. "Louis D. Brandeis: Counsel for the People." In *Eminent American Jews, 1776 to the Present,* 130-157. New York: Frederick Ungar Publishing Co., 1970. 400 pp.

This article is based on the next entry.

————, "Louis D. Brandeis: 'Counsel for the People.'" In *Leaders and Liberals in 20th Century America,* 173-227. New York, Frederick Ungar Publishing Co., 1961. 499 pp.

"Justice Louis D. Brandeis is shown as the chief critic of industrial bigness and social intolerance as well as the idealogical link between the New Freedom and the New Deal," at p. viii.

Martin, Albro. *Enterprise Denied: Origins of the Decline of American Railroads, 1897-1917.* New York: Columbia University Press, 1971. 402 pp.

Brandeis and his influence on the railroad industry before he joined the Supreme Court is described throughout. The book is based on the author's Ph.D. dissertation from Columbia University.

Mason, Alpheus Thomas. *Bureaucracy Convicts Itself. The Ballinger-Pinchot Controversy of 1910.* New York: The Viking Press, 1941. 224 pp.

The controversy began on August 18, 1909, when Louis R. Glavis, an obscure General Land Office agent formally accused Secretary of the Interior Richard A. Ballinger of poor conduct and not being worthy of being a high government official. Naturally, Glavis was then discharged by Ballinger as insubordinate.

A joint congressional investigating committee held hearings on this matter. Brandeis was the counsel for *Collier's Weekly* for a fee of $25,000. The Committee issued thirteen volumes of hearings and reports (majority and minority) as Senate Document 719 (1911) 61st Congress, 3rd Session. Ballinger resigned shortly after the hearings ended.

Miller, Charles A. *The Supreme Court and the Uses of History.* Cambridge, Mass., The Belknap Press of Harvard University Press, 1969. 234 pp.

Brandeis is often referred to and quoted by Miller. He writes, "Justice Brandeis is the outstanding example of a jurist keenly aware of the legal and social functions of the Court, and therefore of the political role that mediates them. At the same time, Justice Brandeis viewed the Court as a teacher to the nation of both scholarly and moral truths," at p. 194.

Moore, Thomas Lane, III. *The Establishment of a "New Freedom" Policy: The Federal Trade Commission, 1912–1918.* Ph.D. diss. University, Ala.: University of Alabama Press, 1980. 312 leaves.

Morris, Lloyd. "Savonarola in Silk." In *Postscript to Yesterday: America: The Last Fifty Years,* 356–368. New York: Random House, 1947. 475 pp.

The chapter surveys Brandeis and his philosophy.

The National Cyclopedia of American Biography. New York: James T. White & Co., Volume 36:1–5 (1950).

It contains a terse biography of Brandeis. An earlier version of this article appeared at Volume C, of the same set at pp. 432–434 (1930).

Nutter, McClennen & Fish: The First Century, 1879–1979. . . . Boston: Privately printed, 1979. 69 pp.

Brandeis' role in forming and developing this law firm is described in chapters 2 and 3. The anonymous author used Mason's *Brandeis–A Free Man's Life* (1946) extensively in detailing the early period in the law firm's history.

Parrish, Michael E. *Felix Frankfurter and His Times: The Reform Years.* New York: The Free Press, 1982. 330 pp.

Parrish describes in detail the relationship between Brandeis and Frankfurter. Is one of the many new biographies of Frankfurter.

Penick, James, Jr. *Progressive Politics and Conservation: The Ballinger-Pinchot Affair.* Chicago: University of Chicago Press, 1968. 207 pp.

It is a more recent re-telling of the Ballinger-Pinchot controversy and Brandeis' role in it. Penick critically reviews the previously published materials on the subject.

Ritchie, Donald A. *James M. Landis: Dean of the Regulators.* Cambridge, Mass.: Harvard University Press, 1980. 267 pp.

Landis was Brandeis' eighth law clerk. Later, he became dean of Harvard Law School and a leading expert in administrative law. Ritchie delves into both Landis' public and private lives.

Roosevelt, Franklin D. *Roosevelt and Frankfurter: Their Correspondence, 1928-1945*. Annotated by Max Freedman. Boston: Little, Brown and Company, 1967. 772 pp.

Brandeis is mentioned often by each correspondent.

Rosen, Paul L. *The Supreme Court and Social Science*. Urbana: University of Illinois Press, 1972. 260 pp.

Rosen examines Brandeis and the Brandeis brief in relation to modern social sciences. See especially pp. 75-101 and 177-182.

Rosenblatt, Bernard A. *Two Generations of Zionism: Historical Recollections of An American Zionist*. New York: Shengold Publishers, Inc., 1967. 286 pp.

Brandeis and the author met in 1912 in New York City. Brandeis became a Zionist in 1912/13. He is mentioned throughout, beginning at p. 55.

Sacher, Harry. "Mr. Justice Brandeis." In *Zionist Portraits and Other Essays*, 63-69. London: Anthony Blond, Ltd., 1959. 355 pp.

This is a brief biography of Brandeis. The essay was originally published in the August 1945 issue of *New Judaea*.

Shapiro, Yonathan. *Leadership of the American Zionist Organization, 1897-1930*. Urbana: University of Illinois Press, 1971. 295 pp.

Brandeis and his supporters in the Zionist movement are discussed throughout, see especially pp. 184-219. Shapiro recounts Brandeis' role in building a powerful Zionist organization that challenged the American Jewish Congress for supremacy of the American Jewish community. This book is based on the author's Ph.D. dissertation, Columbia University, Faculty of Political Science, 1964. 621 pp.

Shulman, Charles E. "Louis D. Brandeis." In *What It Means To Be a Jew*. 79-83. New York: Crown Publishers, Inc., 1960. 256 pp.

Silverstein, Mark. *Constitutional Faiths: Felix Frankfurter, Hugo Black and the Process of Judicial Decision Making*. Ithaca, N.Y.: Cornell University Press, 1984. 234 pp.

The author surveys Brandeis' relationships with Justices Oliver Wendell Holmes and Felix Frankfurter, and Brandeis' constitutional law philosophy.

Sutherland, Arthur E. *The Law at Harvard: A History of Ideas and Men, 1817-1967*. Cambridge, Mass.: The Belknap Press of Harvard University Press, 1967. 408 pp.

Brandeis' law school days are mentioned at pp. 197-199. All of his law clerks graduated from Harvard Law School. Several returned to teach there.

Tugwell, Rexford G. *The Art of Politics: As Practiced by Three Great Americans: Franklin Delano Roosevelt, Luis Muñoz Marin, and Fiorello H. LaGuardia.* Garden City, N.Y.: Doubleday & Company, 1958. 295 pp.

Brandeis' influence on Roosevelt is outlined at pp. 246-248.

Urofsky, Melvin I. *American Zionism from Herzl to the Holocaust.* Garden City, N.Y.: Doubleday & Company, 1975. 538 pp.

Throughout, Brandeis is discussed.

————, *A Voice That Spoke for Justice: The Life and Times of Stephen S. Wise.* Albany, N.Y.: State University of New York Press, 1982. 439 pp.

Brandeis is mentioned throughout this biography of one of the most prominent American rabbis of the twentieth century.

Vorspan, Albert. "Louis Brandeis: From Assimilation to Zion" and "The Supreme Court." In *Giants of Justice,* 22-23, 34-39. New York: Union of American Hebrew Congregations, 1960. 260 pp.

These two chapters are devoted to a basic discussion of Brandeis.

Warren, Earl. "[Address]." In *The Public Papers of Chief Justice Earl Warren,* edited by Henry M. Christman, 89-95. New York, Simon and Schuster, Inc., 1959. 237 pp.

This is Warren's address delivered at the Justice Louis Dembitz Brandeis Centennial Convocation of Brandeis University on November 11, 1956. In addition, the Chief Justice's address was recorded and is available from the American Jewish Archives in Cincinnati as Tape Recording 444.

Weinstein, James. *The Corporate Ideal in the Liberal State: 1900-1918.* Boston: Beacon Press, 1968. 263 pp.

Brandeis is mentioned in passing in several places.

Weizmann, Chaim. *Trial and Error: The Autobiography of Chaim Weizmann.* New York, Harper & Brothers, 1949. 493 pp.

Brandeis is often mentioned in the text. See also *The Letters and Papers of Chaim Wiezmann.* Series A, Letters, vols. 1-23. Various publishers, 1968 to date.

White, G. Edward. "Holmes, Brandeis and the Origins of Judicial Liberalism." Chap. 8 in *The American Judicial Tradition: Profiles of Leading American Judges,* 150-177. New York: Oxford University Press, 1976. 441 pp.

The chapter examines these two justices and their role in fostering liberalism and keeping its "flame" burning during the 1920s.

Williams, Jerre Stockton. *The Supreme Court Speaks.* Austin: University of Texas Press, 1956. 465 pp.

Brandeis' opinions in three leading constitutional law cases are quoted at length. In Part 4, chapter 3, after a short biographical sketch (pp. 216-218), his concurrence in *Whitney v. California* (274 U.S. 357, 372 (1927)) is set out (pp. 219-223). In Part 4, chapter 4, his dissent in *Olmstead v. United States* (277 U.S. 438, 471 (1928)) is reprinted (pp. 225-229) and in Part 4, chapter 5, Brandeis' dissent in *Burnet v. Colorado Oil & Gas Co.* (285 U.S. 393, 405 (1932)) is excerpted, (pp. 231-233).

Wilson, Woodrow. "[Letter, May 5, 1916]." In *The Politics of Woodrow Wilson: Selections from His Speeches and Writings,* edited with an introduction by August Heckscher, 215-233. New York, Harper & Brothers, 1956. 389 pp.

It reproduces President Wilson's letter, dated May 5, 1916, to Senator C. A. Culberson which states his rationale why he nominated Brandeis to the United States Supreme Court.

Wise, Stephen S. "The Brandeis Epoch." Chap. 11 in *Challenging Years,* [autobiography] 182-201. New York. G. P. Putnam's Sons. 1949. 323 pp.

In this chapter of his autobiography, Wise recounts Brandeis, Zionism and the Balfour Declaration. See also two published collections of his letters: *The Personal Letters of Stephen Wise.* Edited by Justine Wise Polier and James Waterman Wise. Boston: Beacon Press 1956, 289 pp; and Stephen S. Wise. *Servant of the People: Selected Letters.* Edited by Carl Hermann Voss. Philadelphia: The Jewish Publications Society of America, 1969. 332 pp.

Wyzanski, Charles Edward, Jr. "Brandeis: The Independent Man." In *Whereas—A Judge's Premises: Essays in Judgment, Ethics and the Law,* 46-64. Boston: Little, Brown and Company, 1965. 312 pp.

This essay was originally delivered as the Brandeis Memorial Lecture at Brandeis University and was published in *Atlantic Monthly* 198(5): 66-72 (November 1956). [As such it is listed in Mersky, at p. 40.] It was, in addition, printed in *Atlantic Essays* (see chapter 4, *infra*).

Judge Wyzanski ranks Brandeis as the second most influential justice on American law after John Marshall, at p. 46. He describes Brandeis' personal moral character and sense of judicial responsibilities.

CHAPTER 4

Essays: These Books Contain Essays on Brandeis
That Were Written by a Person Other Than the Editor of
the Collection

Abramov, S. Z. "Brandeis, Louis Dembitz." In *Encyclopedia of Zionism and Israel,* edited by Raphael Patai, vol. 1, 154-156. New York: Herzl Press/ McGraw Hill, Inc., 1971. 2 vols.

This is a biographical sketch.

Abrams, Richard M. "Brandeis and the Ascendency of Corporate Capitalism." Introduction to reprint of *Other People's Money and How the Bankers Use It,* by Louis Brandeis, vii-xliv. New York: Harper & Row, Publishers, 1967. 152 pp., softcover.

Angoff, Charles, "Louis D. Brandeis: A Footnote." In *The American Judaism Reader: . . . From the Pages of American Judaism,* edited by Paul Kresh, 99-102. New York: Abelard-Schuman, Ltd., 1967. 366 pp.

The article is the personal reminiscences of a man who, at the age of ten, saw Brandeis in Boston and saw him several other times later in his life.

Berman, Hyman. "The Cloakmakers' Strike of 1910." In *Essays on Jewish Life and Thought: Presented in Honor of Salo Wittmayer Baron,* edited by Joseph Leon Blau, 63-94. New York: Columbia University Press, 1959. 458 pp.

Berman discusses the cloakmaker's strike of 1910 and Brandeis' role as a mediator in settling it. Brandeis' tenure as an arbitrator and mediator has never received much attention from historians or his biographers.

Bickel, Alexander M. "Passion and Patience." In *The Faces of Five Decades: Selections from Fifty Years of the New Republic, 1914-1964,* edited by Robert B. Luce, 374-378. New York: Simon & Schuster, 1964. 480 pp.

This article originally appeared in *The New Republic,* November 12, 1956 issue [listed as such in Mersky, at p. 35].

Brandeis, Louis Dembitz. "The Jewish Problem and How to Solve It" and [a biographical sketch of Brandeis]. In *The Zionist Idea: A Historical Analysis and Reader,* edited by Arthur Hertzberg, 517-523, 515-517. Garden City, N.Y.: Doubleday & Company, 1959. 638 pp.

Brandeis wrote this article in 1915.

Cully, Kendig Brubaker. "Louis Dembitz Brandeis: Justice of the Supreme Court." In *Distinguished American Jews,* edited by Philip Henry Lotz, 98-107. Creative Personalities Series, vol. 6. New York: Association Press, 1945. 107 pp.

Feldstein, Thomas M., and Stephen B. Presser. "Louis D. Brandeis." In *The Guide to American Law: Everyone's Legal Encyclopedia,* vol. 2, 145-147. St. Paul, Minn.: West Publishing Co., 1983. 12 vols.

This is a brief biographical portrait of Brandeis.

Freund, Paul A. "Brandeis, Louis Dembitz." In *Dictionary of American Biography,* Supplement Three (1941-1945), 93-100. New York: Charles Scribner's Sons, 1973. 879 pp.

————, "Louis D. Brandeis: An Appreciation." In *Fiftieth Anniversary Convocation . . . ,* by University of Louisville, School of Law, Student Bar Association, 5. 1966. (See chap. 1, *infra.*)

————, "Mr. Justice Brandeis." In *Mr. Justice.* Rev. and enl., edited by Allison Dunham and Philip B. Kurland, 177-202. Chicago: University of Chicago Press, 1964. 344 pp.

In particular, Freund discusses the *Olmstead* decision, 277 U.S. 438 (1928). Originally Brandeis based his opinion on the doctrine of "unclean hands" and avoided the constitutional issue. After Brandeis heard the oral arguments, he switched the grounds for his view and drafted his great dissent.

[The 1956 edition of this work is listed by Mersky, at p. 29.]

Hurst, Willard. "A Tribute." In *Fiftieth Anniversary Convocation . . . ,* by University of Louisville, School of Law, Student Bar Association, 2. 1966. (See chap. 1, *infra.*)

Jackson, Robert H. "Mr. Justice Brandeis: 'Microscope and Telescope'." In *An Autobiography of the Supreme Court,* edited by Alan F. Westin, 233-240. New York: Macmillan Publishing Company, 1963. 475 pp.

The article reproduces Jackson's speech that he delivered at the Brandeis Memorial Colony Dinner on June 23, 1943 (see chap. 1, *infra*) and which was printed in *Vital Speeches* 9:664-667 (1943) [cited by Mersky, at p. 37].

Justice Jackson never served with Brandeis on the Supreme Court, as he was appointed in 1941. But as Solicitor General and Attorney General under President Roosevelt, Jackson saw Justice Brandeis on the bench on many occasions.

Jaffe, Louis L. "Was Brandeis An Activist?" In *Fiftieth Anniversary Convocation* . . . , by University of Louisville, School of Law, Student Bar Association, 6-20. 1966. (See chap. 1, *infra.*)

Konvitz, Milton R. "Louis D. Brandeis." Chap. 10 in *Great Jewish Personalities in Modern Times,* edited by Simon Noveck, 295-316. New York: B'nai B'rith Department of Adult Jewish Education, 1960. 366 pp.

————, "Louis D. Brandeis." In *Molders of the Jewish Mind,* by B'nai B'rith Department of Adult Jewish Education, 219-238. Washington, D.C., 1966. 245 pp.

Kutler, Stanley I. "Louis D. Brandeis." In *Heritage of '76,* edited by Jay P. Dolan, 103-108. South Bend, Ind.: University of Notre Dame Press, 1976. 150 pp.

The book's purpose was to depict Americans who fought for liberty and justice. It was compiled for the Bicentennial Year of 1976.

Levinthal, Louis E. "Louis Dembitz Brandeis." In *Self-Fulfillment Through Zionism: A Study in Jewish Adjustment,* edited by Shlomo Bardin, 86-102. New York: American Zionist Youth Commission, 1943. 128 pp.

Originally, it appeared in *American Jewish Yearbook,* 44:37-52 (1942-43) [cited by Mersky, at p. 38].

"Louis Brandeis." In *Builders of the Homeland.* 3d series, 7-9. Tel Aviv, Israel, Zionist Organization, Youth Department, 1947.

This is a brief treatment of Brandeis.

"Louis Dembitz Brandeis, 1856-1941." In *The International Hebrew Heritage Library,* by the Israeli Publishing Institute, Jerusalem, vol. 8, *Great Jewish Statesmen,* 47-52. Miami: International Book Corp., 1969. 10 vols.

Maslon, Samuel. "A Tribute." In *Fiftieth Anniversary Convocation* . . . , by University of Louisville, School of Law, Student Bar Association, 3-4. 1966. (See chap. 1, *infra.*)

Maslon was one of Brandeis' law clerks.

Mason, Alpheus Thomas. "Brandeis Brief." In *The Guide to American Law: Everyone's Legal Encyclopedia,* vol. 2, 148-150. St. Paul, Minn.: West Publishing Co., 1983. 12 vols.

Mason describes Brandeis' use of non-legal materials in a legal brief.

————, "The Case of the Overworked Laundress." Chap. 12 in *Quarrels That Have Shaped the Constitution*, edited by John A. Garraty, 176-190. New York, Harper & Row, Publishers, 1964. 276 pp.

This is a discussion of *Muller v. Oregon*, 208 U.S. 412 (1908), and Brandeis' role and brief in the case.

————, "Holmes and Brandeis Dissenting." In *Voices in Court: A Treasury of the Bench, the Bar, and the Courtroom*, edited by William Henry Davenport, 228-239. New York: The Macmillan Company, 1958. 588 pp.

The essay contains excerpts from his biography, *Brandeis: A Free Man's Life*, (1946).

————, "Louis D. Brandeis" and [Brandeis' dissent in *Truax Co. v. Corrigan*, 257 U.S. 312, 354, (1921), and his majority opinion in *O'Gorman and Young, Inc. v. Hartford Fire Insurance Co.*, 282 U.S. 251 (1931).] In *The Justices of the United States Supreme Court 1789-1969: Their Lives and Major Opinions*, edited by Leon Friedman and Fred L. Israel, vol. 3, 2043-2059 and 2060-2073. New York: Chelsea House Publishers, 1969. 4 vols.

————, "Mother of a Great American: Frederika Dembitz Brandeis." In *Her Children Call Her Blessed: A Portrait of the Jewish Mother*, edited by Franz Kobler, 212-217. New York: Stephen Daye Press, 1955. 392 pp.

This is taken from his book, *Brandeis: A Free Man's Life* (1946). It consists of a short introduction and excerpts from some of Brandeis' letters to his mother.

Nathanson, Nathaniel L. "The Philosophy of Mr. Justice Brandeis and Civil Liberties Today." In *Six Justices on Civil Rights*, edited by Ronald Rotunda, 134-174. (David C. Baum Memorial Lectures.) Dobbs Ferry, N.Y.: Oceana Publications, Inc., 1983. 211 pp.

This essay written by one of Brandeis' law clerks originally appeared in the *University of Illinois Law Forum* 1979:261-300 (See chap. 2, *infra*).

Parzen, Herbert. "United States of America, Zionism in." In *Encyclopedia of Zionism and Israel*, edited by Raphael Patai, vol. 2, 1163-1171. New York: Herzl Press/McGraw Hill, Inc., 1971. 2 vols.

The selection discusses Brandeis' contribution to Zionism and his supporters, who Parzen calls "Brandeisists."

Richards, Bernard G. "Brandeis and Zionism." In *American Jewish Memoirs: Oral Documentation*, edited by Geoffrey Wigoder, 33-36. Jerusalem: The Hebrew University of Jerusalem, The Institute of Contemporary Jewry, Oral History Division, 1980. 88 pp., softcover.

The article is a transcript of Professor Yonathan Shapiro's 1965 interview of Mr. Richards, an American Jewish leader.

Sachar, Abram L. "Justice Brandeis." In *Jewish Frontier Anthology, 1945–1967*, 116-126. New York: Jewish Frontier Association Inc., 1967, 574 pp.

Written by the president of Brandeis University, this article was originally published in the February 1957 issue of *Jewish Frontier*.

United States Senate Hearings on Brandeis' nomination to the United States Supreme Court; contain the majority and minority reports; and a brief (filed in opposition to his confirmation by Austen G. Fox and Kenneth M. Spence). In *The Supreme Court of the United States: Hearings and Reports on Successful and Unsuccessful Nominations of Supreme Court Justices by the Senate Judiciary Committee, 1916–1972*, compiled by Roy Mersky and J. Myron Jacobstein, vol. 3, 5-174, 175-371, and 99p. Reprint. Buffalo, N.Y.: William S. Hein & Co., 1975.

[The original hearings and report are listed by Mersky, at p. 30.]

Wyzanski, Charles Edward. "Brandeis." In *Atlantic Essays*, by Atlantic Monthly, 180-194. Boston: D.C. Heath & Co., 1958. 463 pp.

This essay originally appeared in *Atlantic Monthly*, 198:66-72 (November 1956) [as such is listed by Mersky, at p. 40]. This essay was also printed in Wyzanski's *Whereas—A Judge's Premises* . . . (See chap. 3, *infra*).

CHAPTER 5

Non-Legal Periodical Articles

Abrahams, Paul P., editor. "Brandeis and Lamont on Finance Capitalism." *Business History Review* 47:72-94 (1973).

This prints an edited transcript of the December 2, 1913 three-hour conversation between Brandeis and Thomas W. Lamont, who was then a partner in J. P. Morgan & Co. Abrahams wrote a short introduction to the article and edited the transcript.

Abrams, Richard M. "Brandeis and the New Haven-Boston & Maine Merger Battle Revisited," *Business History Review* 36:408-430 (1962).

The article relates the struggle over merger of these two railroads. Brandeis opposed it during the years 1907-1909. He wrote about the merger in his books, *Business—A Profession,* and *Other People's Money.*

Agron, Gershon. "Brandeis—Portrait of a Great Zionist." *Zionist Newsletter* 5:16-20 (June 16, 1953).

Agron was the editor of the *Jerusalem Post.*

The American Hebrew [magazine] 139(21): 521-552 (1936).

The entire November 13th issue is devoted to Justice Brandeis. It consists of numerous short tributes praising Brandeis.

Auerbach, Jerold S. "From Rags to Robes: The Legal Profession, Social Mobility and the American Jewish Experience." *American Jewish Historical Quarterly* 66:249-284 (1976).

This article discusses the history of American Jews in the legal profession and the difficulty a Jew had in obtaining a job, during the depression and up until the 1960s and 1970s. Brandeis is mentioned often. He is quoted on the proper role of a lawyer as having, "The moral courage in the face of financial loss and personal ill-will to stand for right and justice," at p. 276.

Badger, William V. "Louis D. Brandeis—Judge, Legal Scholar and Statesman." *Social Science* 34:80–88 (1959).

Badger greatly admires Brandeis as a liberal person, who as a Supreme Court Justice fought for the individual and more personal rights.

Baldwin, Roger. "Affirmation of Democracy." *Jewish Frontier* 3(10): 10–11 (November 1936).

————, "Justice Brandeis and the Bill of Rights." *Herzl Institute Bulletin,* 3(5): 1 (October 30, 1966).

It is an excerpt of a speech Baldwin gave at the Herzl Institute, New York City on October 2, 1966. Is listed also in chap. 8, *infra.*

Ben-Gurion, David. " A Month in a Flying Clipper: I Return Home the Long Way Round." *Jewish Observer & Middle East Review* 13(7): 21–24 (February 14, 1964).

This is Installment 25 in the serialization of Ben-Gurion's "On the Road to the Army and the State." In this article he discussed his 1941 trip, Brandeis and Zionism.

Ben-Zvi, Samuel. "The Kind of an Israel Brandeis Wanted to See." *Israel Horizons* 10(10): 17–19 (December 1962).

The author discusses his meeting with Brandeis in 1941 in Washington, D.C.

Berger, Elmer. "Disenchantment of a Zionist." *Middle East Forum,* April 1962, 1–8.

Berger examines Brandeis, the 1920 London and 1921 Cleveland conferences, and Zionism.

Berlin, George L. "The Brandeis-Weizmann Dispute." *American Jewish Historical Quarterly* 60:37–68 (1970).

The article deals with the dispute between those two men in 1920–21 over the position American Jews should take on the issue of Zionism.

Bernstein, Philip S. "The Spirit of Louis D. Brandeis–His Moral Legacy." *Congress Weekly* 23(15): 6–8 (April 23, 1956).

This is a transcript of the speech he gave at the American Jewish Congress Convention in New York City (April 12–15, 1956) to commemorate the centennial of Brandeis' birth.

Beth, Loren P. "The Supreme Court and the Future of Judicial Review." *Political Science Quarterly* 76:11–23 (1961).

Brandeis is discussed on pp. 16–17. The author states that all Justices since 1937 were influenced by Holmes and Brandeis, at p. 16.

Biddle, Francis. "The Friendship of Holmes and Brandeis." *Atlantic Monthly* 216:86-91 (December 1965).

The author was Holmes' law clerk in 1911-1912, which was before Brandeis joined the court. The friendship with Holmes developed when Brandeis joined the Supreme Court in 1916. Their philosophies of law and life were similar.

Bolner, James. "Mr. Chief Justice Vinson and the Communist Controversy: A Reassessment." *Register of the Kentucky Historical Society* 66:378-391 (1968).

Bolner states the "orthodox" account that Holmes and Brandeis created the theoretical basis of the modern, liberal view of constitutional law and that Vinson (Chief Justice of the Supreme Court, 1946-1953) subverted their work. The author concedes while this view is basically accurate, it does a great injustice to Vinson.

Brandeis, Louis D. "Remarkable Interview with Louis D. Brandeis." *The Jewish Advocate (Boston)* 13(14): 1, 8 (December 9, 1910).

This was the first interview that Brandeis granted to a Jewish newspaper on the subject of Jewish matters and concerns. It has been reproduced in various periodicals.

Cahn, Edmond. "Louis D. Brandeis—As A Jurist." *Congress Weekly* 23(15): 10-12 (April 23, 1956).

Conroy, George R. "Schiff and Brandeis." *Truth,* April 18, 1914.

Cover, Robert. "The Framing of Justice Brandeis: A Political Conspiracy Comes Unraveled." *New Republic* 186:17-21 (May 5, 1982). Reprinted in *New York Law Journal* 188(4): 2 (July 7, 1982).

This article, written by a Yale University law professor, is a forceful defense of Brandeis. It is a strong critique of Murphy's book *Brandeis/ Frankfurter Connection* and a damnation of the *New York Times* and Oxford University Press. Professor Cover claims that people followed Brandeis because he was the dominant intellect and committed person of our times.

Davis, L. J. "Other People's Money: How Justice Brandeis Almost Ruined the Country." *Harpers* 268:62-64 (February 1984).

Davis criticizes Brandeis' philosophy of economics as detailed in his book *Other People's Money.* He says Brandeis mistakenly identified J. P. Morgan as *the* "enemy." Davis believes Morgan's economic view was right and Brandeis' was wrong.

Dawson, Nelson, L. "Curbing Leviathan: The Social Philosophy of Louis D. Brandeis." *Register of the Kentucky Historical Society* 77:30-45 (1979).

Dawson chronicles one of Kentucky's most distinguished citizens and his lifelong opposition to bigness.

————, "Louis D. Brandeis, Felix Frankfurter and Franklin D. Roosevelt: The Origins of a New Deal Relationship." *American Jewish History* 68:32–42 (1978).

The article discusses these three men and their interaction during the New Deal.

————, "Louis D. Brandeis, George Gilder and the Nature of Capitalism." *The Historian* 47:72–85 (November 1984).

Dawson calls George Gilder, "an articulate supply side economist, is a brilliant representative of neo-conservation," at p. 73, while Dawson characterizes Brandeis as "defending the public against the depredations of businessmen," at p. 73. Dawson contrasts and examines these two men's philosophy and conceptions of capitalism and concludes they are in fundamental agreement.

De Haas, Jacob. "Brandeis-Zionist." *The New Palestine* 21(5): 38 (November 6, 1931).

————, "Brandeis at Seventy-Five." *The Modern View*, 1933, 2, 20.

————, "The Fact-Finder." *The New Palestine* 31(4): 9 (November 8, 1940).

————, [Headline reads:] "First Jew Sworn in as Supreme Court Justice." [Subheadline reads:] "People's Advocate, Zionist Leader." *The Jewish Advocate (Boston)* 24(15): 1, 2 (June 8, 1916).

————, "Louis Dembitz Brandeis—Zionist." *The Jewish Tribune* 89(20): 5, 17 (November 12, 1926).

The article tells of their first meeting and the incidents that led to Brandeis' interest in Zionism. The issue also contains five pages of short tributes to the Justice. [Mersky, at p. 36, listed the month as "July."]

DeSala Pool, Tamar. "L'Fee Daati." *Hadassah Newsletter* 22(3): 5 (December 1941–January 1942).

Dinnerstein, Leonard. "Jews and The New Deal." *American Jewish History* 72:461–476 (1983).

Brandeis is mentioned several times.

Douglas, William O. "Kibbutz: 'A Force Felt the World Over'." *Israel Horizons* 11(1): 7–8 (January 1963).

Douglas gave this speech on December 15, 1962. He talked about the Kibbutz Ein Hashofet (The Well of The Judge) and Brandeis' philosophy.

Duffus, R. L. "Brandeis, at 75, Is Still the Fighter: Humane, Liberal, Well Informed and Mercilessly Logical, the Justice Has Revealed His Intellectual Stature." *New York Times Magazine,* November 8, 1931: 3, 20.

————, "Brandeis: Crusader At Eighty: On the Supreme Bench He Continues His Fight for the 'Little Man,' and for the American Democracy in Which He Still Believes." *New York Times Magazine,* November 8, 1936, 4, 24.

————, "Brandeis, 82 Today, Rounds Out a Philosophy: Views He Has Championed So Long Guide Him Still." *New York Times Magazine,* November 13, 1938, 3, 26.

Durham, Allison. Book review: "The Supreme Court: The Legacy of Brandeis, Holmes and Stone. Books by Alpheus T. Mason and Samuel T. Konefsky." *Saturday Review,* 39:13-15, 33 (December 15, 1956.)

This book review contains only a short discussion of Justice Stone. It is mainly about Brandeis and Holmes.

Engelbourg, Saul. "Edward A. Filene: Merchant, Civic Leader, and Jew." *American Jewish Historical Quarterly* 66:106-122 (1976).

Brandeis is mentioned a few times and only in passing. He did legal work for Filene's Department Store. In 1900, Brandeis, Filene and several others founded the Public Franchise League to regulate mass transit and public utilities.

Ernst, Morris L. "The Unforgettable Justice Brandeis." *Readers' Digest* 73:65-70 (July 1958).

The author recalls his relationship with Brandeis and discusses him as a human being, rather than as a Titan. Ernst greatly admired Brandeis.

Evans, Elizabeth Glendower. "Justice Brandeis in the Intimacy of His Home." *The Jewish Advocate: Connecticut Hebrew Record Edition,* November 13, 1931: pt. 2, p. 8.

Feingold, Henry L. " 'Courage First and Intelligence Second': The American Jewish Secular Elite, Roosevelt and the Failure to Rescue." *American Jewish History* 72:424-460 (1983).

Brandeis is mentioned often. The article mainly discusses the Jewish secular community and its internal struggles.

————, See Urofsky, *Zionism: An American Experience, infra.*

Fox, Maier Bryan. "Labor Zionism in America: The Challenge of the 1920s." *American Jewish Archives* 35:53-71 (1983).

Brandeis is spoken of several times.

Fraenkel, Osmond K. "Brandeis and the Changing Economic Order." *Jewish Frontier* 3(10): 6–9 (November 1936).

This is part of a special issue written to honor Brandeis on his eightieth birthday.

Frank, John P. "Brandeis's [*sic*] Successor: Free Speech and William O. Douglas." *New Republic* 182:17–19 (February 2, 1980).

The article is mainly about Douglas, written by one of Douglas' former law clerks. He attempts to show a tie-in between the two justices and that Douglas was the logical successor. Douglas succeeded Brandeis on the Supreme Court in 1939.

———, "Holmes and Brandeis: Civil Rights, 1946." *Twice a Year* 14–15:481–485 (1946–1947).

The political views of the two men are examined. What was once their dissenting position became the majority view after World War II.

Frankfurter, Felix. "A Tribute from Justice Frankfurter." *Congress Weekly* 23(15): 12 April 23, 1956).

This is merely three paragraphs that the editor took out of a letter Frankfurter wrote to the periodical about Brandeis.

Freund, Paul A. "The Evolution of a Brandeis Dissent." *Manuscripts* 10:18–25, 34 (Spring 1958).

Professor Freund used a portion of his essay on Brandeis that appeared in *Mr. Justice* edited by Dunham and Kurland to write this article. In it, Freund describes Brandeis' epic dissent in the *Olmstead* case (277 U.S. 428, 471 (1928)) and how the Justice switched the grounds for his opinion from "unclean hands" to constitutional ones after he heard the oral arguments.

Especially interesting are the reproductions of Brandeis' handwritten drafts of his opinion and his corrections of the printer's proofs, at pp. 22–23.

———, "Justice Brandeis: A Law Clerk's Remembrance, Historical Reminiscence." *American Jewish History* 68:7–18 (1978).

Freund describes his year (1932–1933) as Brandeis' law clerk as well as Brandeis' apartment, Sunday teas and Zionism.

———, "The Liberalism of Justice Brandeis." *American Jewish Archives* 10:3–11 (1958).

This essay was originally delivered as an address at a meeting of the American Historical Association in St. Louis on December 28, 1956.

————, Untitled. [An excerpt of his address on Brandeis, given at the Thirteenth Anniversary of the founding of Brandeis University.] *Boston Sunday Globe*, (October 22, 1978), A4.

He retraces Brandeis' career. This is also listed in chap. 8, *infra*.

Friesel, Evyatar. "Brandeis' Role in American Zionism Historically Reconsidered." *American Jewish History* 69:34-65 (1979). Photographs of Justice Brandeis, pp. 59-65.

Brandeis is discussed throughout the article. His period of dominance in the American Zionist movement is 1914-1921. Friesel says that American Zionism until 1930 may be called "Brandeiscentric," at p. 34.
　　This article was reprinted in *Solidarity and Kinship: Essays on American Zionism in Memory of Dewey David Stone*, edited by Nathan M. Kaganoff. Waltham, Mass.: American Jewish Historical Society, 1980, at pp. 56-87.

————, "Jacob H. Schiff Becomes a Zionist: A Chapter in American-Jewish Self Definition, 1907-1917." *Studies in Zionism* 5:55-92 (1982).

Schiff was a man of great wealth, an outstanding philanthropist, and a leader of the German-American community. For various reasons, he and Brandeis disagreed and battled over the direction the American Zionist movement should take, and over the Balfour Declaration.

Gal, Allon. "Brandeis's [*sic*] View on the Upbuilding of Palestine, 1914-1923." *Studies in Zionism* 6:211-240 (1982).

The article discusses Brandeis' fight and disagreement with Chaim Weizmann, the European leader, over the direction that Zionism and Palestine should take. The American leaders, Brandeis and his supporters, lost but remained committed to Zionism.

————, "In Search of a New Zion: New Light on Brandeis' Road to Zionism." *American Jewish History* 68:19-31 (1978).

Gal discusses the years 1910-1913 when Brandeis became a Zionist.

Gardner, Woodford L., Jr. "Kentucky Justices on the U.S. Supreme Court." *Register of the Kentucky Historical Society* 70:121-142 (1972).

A brief treatment of Brandeis is found at pp. 135-136. Brandeis is one of the eight Kentucky-born United States Supreme Court justices.

Gartner, Lloyd P. Book review: "Leadership of the American Zionist Organization, 1897-1930." *American Jewish Historical Quarterly* 62:76-79 (1972).

This is a book review of Shapiro's book of the same title (see chap. 3, *infra*).

Geffen, David. "A Letter from the Emek. Mordechai Bentov to Justice Louis Brandeis, 1934." *Forum,* no. 37: 169–174 (Spring 1980).

Geffen introduces a letter, dated May 30, 1934, written by Bentov to Brandeis describing life on a kibbutz and the progress being made on it, then reproduces the letter.

Geller, Stuart Mitchell. "Why Did Louis D. Brandeis Choose Zionism?" *American Jewish Historical Quarterly* 62:383–400 (1973).

Geller investigates Brandeis' decision to become a Zionist. Also, Geller discusses Brandeis' appointment by President Wilson to the United States Supreme Court.

Goedecke, Robert. "Holmes, Brandeis, and Frankfurter: Differences in Pragmatic Jurisprudence." *Ethics* 74:83–96 (1964).

Goedecke describes the three men's differences, philosophies and interactions.

Goldberg, Hillel. "Louis D. Brandeis, The Jew." *Intermountain Jewish News Literary Supplement (Denver, Colo.).* 1(2): 1–19 (July 22, 1983). Oversized.

The entire issue is a glowing tribute to the Justice.

Goldman, Sheldon. "In Defense of Justice: Some Thoughts on Reading Professor Mendelson's 'Mr. Justice Douglas and Government by the Judiciary'." *Journal of Politics* 39:146–158 (1977).

Goldman calls Brandeis one of the great liberal justices. Mendelson took issue, see his response in *Journal of Politics* 39:159–165 (1977) (listed *infra*).

Goldman, Solomon. "Character and Destiny." *The New Palestine* 32(3): 7–8 (October 17, 1941).

This is an obituary of Brandeis.

———, "Justice Louis D. Brandeis—As American and Jew." *The New Palestine* 31(4): 7–8 (November 4, 1940).

Grose, Peter. "Louis Brandeis, Arthur Balfour and a Declaration That Made History: Is the story of how a chance encounter on Cape Cod led to one of the most consequential documents of the 20th century." *Moment* 8(10): 27–31, 34–39 (November 1983).

Hadassah Newsletter 22(3): (December 1941–January 1942).

This issue contains five articles and an editorial on Justice Brandeis. Individual entries have been listed for each article, *infra*. Includes a full page photograph of Brandeis.

Halpern, Ben. "The Americanization of Zionism, 1880-1930." *American Jewish History* 69:15-33 (1979).

The article is a short history of the Zionist movement in the United States. Brandeis is named often, especially on pp. 24-26.

———, "Brandeis and the Origins of the Balfour Declaration." *Studies In Zionism* 7:71-100 (1983).

Halpern presents another view of Brandeis' involvement in the formulation in 1917 of the Balfour Declaration. Originally, most commentators believed Brandeis played a key role, both as a Jewish leader and as a close adviser of President Wilson. However, more recent accounts downplay his role and upgrade Colonel Edward M. House's (one of President Wilson's key advisers).

———, "Brandeis' Way to Zionism." *Midstream* 17(8): 3-13 (October 1971).

The article recounts Brandeis' conversion to Zionism.

Hapgood, Norman. "Brandeis and Tomorrow." *Jewish Frontier* 3(10): 11-12 (November 1936).

Harris, Barbara Ann. "The Zionist Rhetoric of Louis Dembitz Brandeis." *Western Speech* 35:199-209 (1971).

Harris says Brandeis delivered thirty-four extant speeches on Zionism. She classified twenty as political, given during the period 1913-1916; six were organizational, given at the London Conference, July 1920; and eight were economic in nature, delivered in the time period 1921-1929. Unfortunately, Harris does not list the speeches individually.

Hodess, J. "L. D. Brandeis [Obituary]." *The New Judaea* (London) 18(5): 5-7 (October 1941).

"Homage to Louis D. Brandeis." *Jewish Frontier* 3(10): 6-27 (November 1936).

This contains eight short articles on him. Individual entries have been made for each article, *infra*.

Jackson, Robert H. "The Creed of a Modern Liberal." *Jewish Frontier* 10(7): 7-10 (July 1943).

It is a speech delivered at the Louis D. Brandeis Memorial Colony Dinner held under the auspices of the Jewish National Fund at the Hotel Commodore, New York City on June 23, 1943. [Listed by Mersky, at p. 37, as appearing in *Vital Speeches of the Day* with a different title.] It was reprinted in *An Autobiography of the Supreme Court*, edited by Alan F. Westin (1963) (see chap. 4, *infra*).

Jacobs, Rose G. "Justice Brandeis: Friend of Hadassah." *Hadassah Newsletter* 17(2): 2 (November 1936).

Kallen, Horace M. "Philospher of Americanism." *Jewish Frontier* 3(10): 12-13 (November 1936).

Kanter, Alex. "I Knew Brandeis: Some Personal Recollections." *Jewish Digest* 9(8): 31-34 (May 1964).

Kanter discusses his meeting with Brandeis in Minneapolis before World War I. They corresponded thereafter for thirty years.

Katz, Irving. "Henry Lee Higginson vs. Louis Dembitz Brandeis: A Collision Between Tradition and Reform." *New England Quarterly* 41:67-81 (1968).

In the 1910s Higginson was Boston's leading investment banker. He opposed Brandeis' reform efforts and his nomination to the United States Supreme Court.

Kaukas, Dick. "The Law and Louis Brandeis." *Louisville Times. Scene Magazine*, February 14, 1981: 3-5.

This is a brief article on the Justice. I supplied him with several articles and leads. The magazine's cover is a full-page photograph of a serious-looking Brandeis attired in his judicial robe.

Keating, Kenneth B. "The Lawyer Statesman." *Herzl Institute Bulletin* 3(5): 1, 6 (October 30, 1966).

Prints an excerpt of a speech Keating gave at the Herzl Institute, New York City on October 2, 1966. (This is listed also in chap. 8, *infra*.)

Knee, Stuart E. "Jewish Non-Zionism in America and Palestine Commitment 1917-1941." *Jewish Social Studies* 39:209-226 (1977).

Knee discusses both the American-Zionist and the Non-Zionist movements during the time period 1917-1941.

Kraines, Oscar. "Brandeis and Scientific Management." *Publications of the American Jewish Historical Society* 41:41-60 (1951).

Brandeis, in opposing higher freight rates, testified before the Interstate Commerce Commission in 1910 that scientific management (efficiency) would enable railroad companies to increase wages and earn more money at the same time.

———, "Brandeis' Philosophy of Scientific Management." *Western Political Quarterly* 13:191-201 (1960).

This article analyzes Brandeis' introduction of the concept of scientific management and his testimony on this topic before the Interstate Commerce Commission on November 21, 1910.

Krislov, Samuel. "Church, State and Kashruth: Some Hidden Dimensions of Pluralism." *Jewish Social Studies* 25:174–185 (1963).

The author comments that, "It is interesting to note that Jewish judges have, in general, not participated in decisions on *kashruth* questions. Justice Brandeis disqualified himself in the *Hygrade Provision Co. v. Sherman*, 266 U.S. 497 (1925) case, as did Judge Lehman on *People v. Gordon*, 283 N.Y. 705, 28 N.E. 2d 717, affirming 258 App. Div. 421, 16 N.Y. Supp. 2d 833 (1940) at p. 184.

Landis, James M. "Mr. Justice Brandeis: A Law Clerk's View." *Publications of the American Jewish Historical Society* 46:467–473 (1957).

Landis was Brandeis' law clerk during the October 1925 term. He gave this article originally as a speech at the fifty-fifth annual meeting of said organization.

Lipsky, Eleazar. "Brandeis and Zionism." *Congress Bi-Weekly* 40(14): 15–16 (December 14, 1973).

He retells the Brandeis-Weizmann struggle.

McCraw, Thomas K. "Louis D. Brandeis Reappraised." *American Scholar* 54:525–536 (1985).

Professor McCraw critically reviews Brandeis' economic views as a lawyer and as a Supreme Court Justice and the recent demythication of him by several biographers. In the course of his research, McCraw discovered Brandeis to be "so wrong in so many aspects of his economic thought," at p. 535, yet calls him a great man, at p. 536.

Madison, Charles A. "Louis D. Brandeis: Jew and Zionist." *Chicago Jewish Forum* 10:262–267 (1952).

Mahoney, Joseph F. "Backsliding Convert: Woodrow Wilson and the 'Seven Sisters.'" *American Quarterly* 18:71–80 (1966).

The article is mostly about Woodrow Wilson, however, the author describes Brandeis' influence on Wilson, beginning with their August 1912 meeting. The "seven sisters" refer to seven New Jersey antitrust statutes enacted in 1913 during Wilson's term as governor of New Jersey.

Mauskopf, Manfried. "Brandeis' Role in American Zionism." *Jewish Horizon* 16(10): 15–18 (June 1954).

Mauskopf recounts Brandeis' contributions to the American Zionist movement.

Melamed, Samuel M. "Justice Brandeis and Dr. Weizmann." *The Jewish Criterion* 72(2): 3–4, 53 (May 18, 1928).

Brandeis and Weizmann took opposite positions on the issue of Zionism. Melamed sums up their positions.

————, "L. D. Brandeis and Chaim Weizmann." *The Reflex* 2(5): 1-10 (May 1928).

This is a quite bitter attack on Brandeis and his role in the American Zionist movement. Dr. Melamed favors Chaim Weizmann as a better person.

Mendelson, Wallace. "A Response to Professor Goldman." *Journal of Politics* 39:159-165 (1977).

Professor Mendelson discusses Brandeis on pp. 159-161 and makes him less of a liberal than one might assume. His article refers to Sheldon Goldman's article in the *Journal of Politics* 39:148-158 (1977) (listed *infra*). Goldman calls Brandeis one of the great liberal justices.

Merritt, James. "Mr. Justice Brandeis: The Law Refocused." *Louisville Magazine* 27(8): 33-36, 65. (August 1976).

This is one part of a two-part article on Brandeis. The other part was written by Anne Ogden, listed *infra*.

Michael, Jerome. "Mr. Justice Brandeis." *Jewish Frontier* 3(10): 18-21 (November 1936).

Miller, Neville. "Justice Brandeis and the University of Louisville School of Law." *Filson Club History Quarterly* 34:156-159 (1960).

It is a transcript of the speech given by the former dean of the Law School on April 18, 1959 at the dedication of the Louis Dembitz Brandeis Seminar Room at the University of Louisville School of Law. Miller relates many of Brandeis' contributions to the law school.

Mittell, Sherman Fabian. "Brandeis." *Journal of Adult Education* 12:142-146 (1940).

This is a glowing tribute to the Justice, which was written one year before Brandeis died.

Morris, Jeffrey B. "The American Jewish Judge: An Appraisal on the Occasion of the Bicentennial." *Jewish Social Studies* 38:195-223 (1976).

Brandeis is discussed throughout, especially at pp. 205-207.

Moskowitz, Henry. "An Army of Striking Cloakmakers: Reminiscences, 1910-1916." *Jewish Frontier* 3(10): 14-16 (November 1936).

Nathanson, Nathaniel L. "Mr. Justice Brandeis: A Law Clerk's Recollection of the October Term, 1934." *American Jewish Archives* 15:6-16 (1963).

It is a reverent tribute to his former boss.

Neumann, Emanuel. "Louis D. Brandeis, Zionist." *The New Palestine* 31(4): 5 (November 8, 1940).

The New Palestine. 36(33): [entire issue] (November 13, 1936).

The issue contains several tributes to Justice Brandeis.

Newland, Chester A. "Innovation in Judicial Technique: The Brandeis Opinion." *Southwestern Social Science Quarterly* 42:22-31 (1961).

The author credits Brandeis with the fundamental change in the format of Supreme Court opinions which now routinely cite to extra-judicial sources such as law review articles.

The innovation began with Brandeis' brief in the *Muller* case (208 U.S. 412 (1908)). Other justices followed Brandeis' lead after he joined the court in 1916. The high point may be the famous footnote 11 in *Brown v. Board of Education* (347 U.S. 483 (1954)) which used sociological and psychological studies to overturn the "separate but equal" legal doctrine of segregated schools.

This article was reprinted as a pamphlet.

Ogden, Anne. "Mr. Justice Brandeis: The Man Remembered." *Louisville Magazine* 27(8): 33-36, 64 (August 1976).

This is one part of a two-part article on Brandeis. The other part was written by James Merritt, listed *infra*.

Panitz, Esther. "Louis Dembitz Brandeis and the Cleveland Conference." *American Jewish Historical Quarterly* 65:140-162 (1975).

During 1920-1921, Brandeis and Weitzmann fought bitterly over the direction that the Zionist movement would take. The American (Brandeis') view lost. This article is based upon a talk she gave at the 1967 Herzl Conference in New York City.

———, "'Washington Versus Pinsk': The Brandeis-Weizmann Dispute." *Herzl Yearbook* 8:77-94 (1978).

Is another re-telling of their epic struggle. The volume is subtitled *Essays in American Zionism, 1917-1948*, edited by Melvin I. Urofsky.

Parzen, Herbert. "Brandeis and the Balfour Declaration." *Herzl Yearbook* 5:309-350 (1963).

Parzen surveys the history of the formation of the Declaration, and Brandeis' role.

Press, Aric. "Secrets of Two Brethren." *Newsweek*, February 22, 1982, 65-66.

Press discusses the Murphy book and the Brandeis-Frankfurter relationship.

Pringle, Henry F. Book review: "A Man Who Was Sure of His Facts. *Brandeis: A Free Man's Life. . . ." Saturday Review of Literature* 29(38): 7–8 (September 21, 1946).

It is a positive book review of Mason's 1946 biography of Brandeis.

Pronin, Malka. "Portrait of a Jew as American." *Jewish Frontier* 3(10): 22–27 (November 1936).

Besides the text, the article reproduces the only portrait which Brandeis posed for, painted by Frank H. Tompkins in 1888.

Read, James Morgan, "Which Way Zionism?" *New Republic* 112:667–670 (1945).

The article was written at the end of World War II at the beginning of the renewed discussion of Israel as a homeland for Jews. Brandeis' role in the pre–World War II discussion is set out.

Richards, Bernard G. "When Mr. Brandeis Met With the Opposition: A Dramatic Chapter of American Jewish History is Told in an Unpublished Letter of Louis D. Brandeis to Louis Lipsky. [Dated May 31, 1916, Boston.]" *American Zionist* 55:16–18 (May 1965).

The subtitle describes the article.

Rittenberg, Louis. "Louis D. Brandeis: Lover of Humanity. Spiritual Estimate of an Apostle of Social Justice at Eighty." *The American Hebrew* 139(21): 526–527, 545–547, and 552 (1936).

Rockaway, Robert A. "Louis Brandeis on Detroit." *Michigan Jewish History* 17(1): 17–19 (July 1977).

This short article is based on a letter dated October 10, 1914, Brandeis wrote to his brother about his trip to Detroit, and anti-semitism there. The brief letter is reproduced. The original letter is in the University of Louisville Law Library's collection of Brandeis papers.

Rooney, Miriam Theresa. "Law as An Instrument of Social Policy: The Brandeis Theory." *New Scholasticism* 22:34–89 (January 1948).

In this rather lengthy philosophical exposition of Brandeis' jurisprudential beliefs, Rooney uses Brandeis' articles, speeches and Supreme Court writings to illustrate that Brandeis used law as an instrument in the struggle for freedom and justice for the common man.

Rosensohn, Samuel J. "Brandeis—Prophet and Realist." *Hadassah Newsletter* 17(2): 7–8 and 10 (November 1936).

Rudavsky, David. "Louis D. Brandeis at the London International Zionist Conference of 1920." *Yivo Annual of Jewish Social Science* 15:145–165 (1974).

The article chronicles Brandeis' role in that meeting. Brandeis met Weizmann in 1919, while touring Palestine. They opposed each other over the direction Zionism should take.

Rudin, A. James. "Brandeis and De Haas: Two Conflicting Styles of Jewish Leadership." *Judaism* 24:296-305 (1975).

The author argues that De Haas' "middle years" consisted of loyal service to Justice Brandeis. Between April and November 1917 they were in almost daily correspondence yet they differed greatly on the Balfour Declaration.

Sachar, Abram L. "Brandeis: His impact on the Jewish Scene." *Jewish Frontier* 24(2): 5-9 (February 1957).

This is the transcript of a speech given by Sachar, the President of Brandeis University, before a meeting of the Zionist Organization of America in Washington, D.C. in October 1956.

Sacher, Harry. "Mr. Justice Brandeis: Zionist Profiles." *The New Judaea* 22(1): 9-11 (October 1945).

Sacher, Howard Morley. See Urofsky, *Zionism: An American Experience, infra.*

Schmidt, Sarah. "Horace M. Kallen and the 'Americanization' of Zionism— In Memoriam." *American Jewish Archives* 28:59-73 (1976).

Brandeis is discussed in his relationship to American Zionism, at pp. 64-72.

————, "Horace M. Kallen and the 'Progressive' Reform of American Zionism." *Midstream* 22(10): 14-23 (December 1976).

Brandeis is referred to in connection with the issue of Zionism at pp. 16-18 and following.

————, "The *Parushim*: A Secret Episode in American Zionist History." *American Jewish Historical Quarterly* 65:121-139 (1975).

This is the story of a secret Zionist society and reform movement called the *Parushim*, started by Horace M. Kallen. Brandeis is named throughout regarding his role in the Zionist movement and the Society.

————, "The Zionist Conversion of Louis D. Brandeis." *Jewish Social Studies* 37:18-34 (1975).

Reviews the literature on Brandeis' decision to become a Zionist and focuses on the part Horace Kallen played in the event and Brandeis' espousal of Zionism.

Schwartz, Sulamith. "Brandeis' Road to Zionism." *Hadassah Newsletter* 22(3): 12-13 (December 1941-January 1942).

Shapiro, Yonathan. "American Jews in Politics: The Case of Louis D. Brandeis." *American Jewish Historical Quarterly* 55:199-211 (1965).

Discusses Brandeis, President Woodrow Wilson, the Zionist movement, and the organized American Jewish community.

Sherman, C. Bezalel. "Brandeis and the First American Jewish Congress." *Jewish Frontier* 34(6): 10-16 (June 1967).

Brandeis was involved in the founding of the American Jewish Congress. However, the leaders of the first conference rejected Brandeis' ideas and suggestions. On becoming a Justice of the Supreme Court, he resigned from the organization. This article is based on Sherman's address given at Herzl Institute's 1966 symposium remembering the death of Justice Brandeis. (See chap. 8 "Speeches about Brandeis" for a listing of all the speeches delivered at the Conference.)

Shulman, Charles E. "Louis D. Brandeis—Exemplar of American Zionism." *American Zionist* 57:9-10 (December 1966).

Siegan, Bernard H. "The Decline and Fall of Economic Freedom." *Reason* 12(9): 48-51 (January 1981).

The author's thrust is that the United States Supreme Court in three decisions mandated due process in the economic sphere and approved of regulation of business, a stance with which Siegan is not happy. One case was Brandeis' lengthy dissent in *New State Ice Co. v. Liebmann*, 285 U.S. 262, 280 (1932).

This short article is adapted from Siegan's book, *Economic Liberties and the Constitution* (1980).

Simon, Julius. "The System of Brandeis." *Palestine Review* 6:107-108 (November 2, 1941).

This is one of the eulogies of Brandeis spoken at a memorial meeting at Ein Hashofet, the Israeli kibbutz named for Justice Brandeis.

Siskin, Edgar E. "Mr. Justice Brandeis: A Rabbi's Recollection." *American Jewish Archives* 18:129-132 (1966).

Siskin discusses a meeting he had with Brandeis. His version differs somewhat with Professor Nathanson's telling of the meeting (*American Jewish Archives* 15:6, at 15 (1963)).

Sobeloff, Simon E. "American and Jew." *Congress Weekly* 23(15): 8-10 (April 23, 1956).

"The Spirit of Louis D. Brandeis." *Congress Weekly* 23(15): 6-12 (April 23, 1956).

The article contains three speeches, by Philip S. Bernstein, Simon E. Soboloff, Edmond Cahn, and three paragraphs written by Felix Frankfurter on Justice Brandeis. Each is listed separately herein.

Stern, Ellen Norman. "Brandeis: The Great Reformer." *World Over: A Magazine for Young People* 34(6): 6-7 (December 15, 1972).

This article is one in the magazine's Great Personalities Series.

Syrkin, Marie, "Brandeis and Zionism." *Jewish Frontier* 3(10): 28-30 (November 1936).

Besides the text, the article reproduces a photograph of Brandeis taken in July 1935 in his study at his summer home in Chatham, Mass.

Szajkowski, Zosa. "Concord and Discord in American Jewish Overseas Relief, 1914-1924." *Yivo Annual of Jewish Social Science* 14:99-158 (1969).

Szajkowski relates the part Brandeis played in the support of the American Jewish Overseas Relief Fund.

Szold, Henrietta. "When Brandeis Came to Zionism." *Hadassah Newsletter* 22(3): 9-10 (December 1941-January 1942).

Teller, Judd L. "America's Two Zionist Traditions: Brandeis and Weizmann." *Commentary* 20:343-352 (1955).

Describes the two men's positions on Zionism and their split.

Ticktin, Harold. Book review: "Louis D. Brandeis: His Life and Letters." *Congress Bi-Weekly* 39(2): 20-22 (January 28, 1972).

Ticktin reviews Urofsky's *Mind of One Piece* and volume 1 of *The Letters of Brandeis* (Urofsky and Levy, editors).

————, " 'The Jewish Seat' (cont'd.)." *Congress Bi-Weekly* 36(15): 18-20 (December 19, 1969).

He rebuts Beryl Harold Levy's article (*Congress Bi-Weekly* 36(13): 3-5 (November 21, 1969)) which attacked the concept of a Jewish seat on the United States Supreme Court.

Toll, William. Book review: "Murphy, The Brandeis/Frankfurter Connection. . . ." *American Jewish Archives* 34:249-252 (1982).

It is a critical review of the Murphy biography.

Tyler, Gus. "Louis D. Brandeis; Way To Jewish Identification." *Herzl Institute Bulletin,* 3(6): 1, 2, and 6 (November 6, 1966).

It is an excerpt of a speech Tyler gave at the Herzl Institute, New York City on October 2, 1966. Also listed in chap. 8, *infra*.

Urofsky, Melvin I. "American Jewish Leadership." *American Jewish History* 70:401–419 (1981).

This is a revised version of a speech Professor Urofsky gave at the General Assembly of the Council of Jewish Federations on November 15, 1980. Brandeis is mentioned briefly throughout the article.

————, "Brandeis and American Zionism." *Reconstructionist* 36:7–13 (May 8, 1970).

Urofsky briefly recounts Brandeis' role in the Zionist movement.

————, "The Conservatism of Mr. Justice Brandeis." *Modern Age* 23:39–48 (1979).

The article is based on a speech Professor Urofsky delivered as the Herman G. Handmaker Memorial Lecture at the University of Louisville Law School in March 1978.

————, "The Emergence of Brandeis as a Zionist." *Midstream* 21:42:58 (January 1975).

He retells Brandeis' acceptance of Zionism in the 1910s.

————, "The Lawyer—Qua-Citizen: The Relevance of Brandeis Today." *Filson Club History Quarterly* 47:5–13 (1973).

This is a glowing tribute to Brandeis. Urofsky calls him a "great man," at p. 5, and further states, "[F]or him, practice of the law and of the duties of a citizen were a well-rounded whole, not divisible pieces. He gave a great deal of his time to public service work, yet he did not neglect his own lucrative practice. He made a great deal of money, so that he would be free to work in those causes in which he believed. He had noble and lofty ideals, but he was a craftsman, . . ." at p. 12.

This article is Urofsky's speech given at the Brandeis Lecture Series at the University of Louisville School of Law on April 3, 1972.

————, "New World, New Zion and New State." *Jewish Observer and Middle East Review* 25(25): 10–11 (June 18, 1976).

The article traces the history of American Jewry and the development of American Zionism. Urofsky refers to Brandeis often in this short article.

————, "Wilson, Brandeis and the Trust Issue, 1912–1914." *Mid-America* 49:3–28 (1967).

Brandeis, before joining the Supreme Court, served as one of President Wilson's key advisers. The issue of trusts brought both men together in the summer of 1912. Professor Urofsky traces the history of their involvement in the anti-monopoly field.

———, "Zionism: An American Experience." *American Jewish Historical Quarterly* 63:215-243 (1974).

Pages 215-230 contain Urofsky's view of Brandeis' role in the American Zionist movement. Following it is a discussion by Henry L. Feingold (pp. 230-238) and by Howard Morley Sacher (pp. 238-243) of Urofsky's theory.

Ussishkin, Menachem. "The Passion for Justice." *Hadassah Newsletter* 22(3): 11-12 (December 1941-January 1942).

In 1936, at a celebration of Brandeis' eightieth birthday in Jerusalem, Ussishkin delivered, in Hebrew, this article as a speech. It was translated into English especially for this issue of the *Hadassah Newsletter*.

Vose, Clement E. "The National Consumers' League and the Brandeis Brief." *Midwest Journal of Political Science* 1:267-290 (1957).

Vose discusses the League, the famous Brandeis Brief, and Brandeis' role as a reformer.

Walsh, Frank P. "An Estimate." *Jewish Frontier* 3(10): 16 (November 1936).

Wolkinson, Benjamin W. "Labor and the Jewish Tradition—A Reappraisal." *Jewish Social Studies* 40:231-238 (1978).

The author states that while Brandeis was a firm opponent of the concept of a closed shop, he favored preferential employment of union members, at p. 234.

Unsigned. "An American Tradition; the Strength of Multiple Loyalties." *Near East Report* 19:137 (August 13, 1975).

Reprints a statement by Brandeis on the concept of multiple national loyalties.

———, "Brandeis and Zionism: Who Used Whom?" *Information Bulletin (American Council for Judaism)* 7(2): 1-3 (March-April 1966).

———, "M. M. Brandeisism in Retrospect." *Palestine Review* 6:108-109. (November 3, 1941).

This article outlines Brandeis' position on Zionism.

———, "Justice Brandeis and Zionism: An Important Part of the Record." *Information Bulletin of the American Council for Judaism*, no. 54: 1-2 (n.d.).

The article recounts the repudiation of Brandeis by the World Zionist leaders at London and Cleveland conferences. The article was reprinted as "When is a Zionist Not a Zionist?" in *American Council for Judaism. Council News* (November 30, 1956).

————, "Justice Goldberg Reaffirms Brandeis Statement on Zionism as Being Compatible with Americanism." *Israel Digest* 8(11): 8 (May 21, 1965).

This is a short excerpt of a speech Goldberg delivered at the annual dinner of the American Israel Public Affairs Committee, Washington, D.C. in early 1965.

————, "A November 'Remember'; Louis D. Brandeis." *Young Judaean: A Magazine for Jewish Youth* 55:15 (November 1966).

————, "Revolutionary Then, Orthodox Now." *Business Week*, no. 1755: 94 (April 20, 1963).

The article briefly describes Brandeis' introduction of the term "scientific management."

————, "The Twelve Great Justices of All Times." *Life* 71(16): 52–59 (October 15, 1971).

The article is based on Blaustein & Mersky's book, *The First Hundred Justices* (1978). Brandeis is one of the twelve listed. There is a picture of him and a short biography on p. 56.

CHAPTER 6

Correspondence to and from Brandeis, in Manuscript Collections

I compiled this chapter from the following:

1. *National Union Catalog of Manuscript Collections* (U.S. Library of Congress) 1959 (the first volume issued) to date (1984 is the latest volume issued).

2. Melvin I. Urofsky and David W. Levy, eds. *The Letters of Louis D. Brandeis* (Albany: State University of New York Press) 5 vols., 1971–1978. A single asterisk (*) indicates that I obtained the listing from their "Cumulative Key to Letter Source Citations," at vol. 5, xxiii–xxix.

3. Two asterisks (**) indicate that I found information in Professors Urofsky's and Levy's correspondence with various archives and libraries they consulted in compiling the above work. They donated their work product to the Archives, William F. Ekstrom Library, University of Louisville, Louisville, Kentucky.

4. *Who Was Who in America* (Wilmette, Ill., Who's Who, Inc.) 9 vols. covering 1607–1985, as indicated by "WWW [volume number] / [page number]" for dead Americans.

5. *Who's Who in America* (Wilmette, Ill., Who's Who, Inc.) vol. 43, 1984–1985, as indicated by "WWA 43 / [page number]" for living Americans.

6. Responses from Manuscript Division librarians to my requests for information.

7. My research in other volumes and sets, and in the Brandeis Papers at the University of Louisville Law Library.

For each entry, I attempted to include eight pieces of information. I was not successful every time, but not for want of trying. The eight are:

1. The individual's first and last name, or corporate entry.

2. His birth and death dates. (In some instances, they varied from source to source.)

3. The number of letters from Justice Brandeis in the manuscript collection.

4. The name of the institution owning the letters, its city and state.

5. The *National Union Catalog of Manuscript Collections'* MS number. However, some collections have not reported their holdings to the Library of Congress.

6. A terse description of the individual's occupation and/or professional achievements. Usually, I took this information from the *National Union Catalog of Manuscript Collections'* listing, or from *Who Was Who in America* or *Who's Who in America.*

7. The volume and page reference in either *Who Was Who in America,* or *Who's Who in America.*

8. Annotation regarding the scope of the collection, etc.

Aaronsohn, Aaron (ca. 1873–1919). Papers: Louis Brandeis File, The Central Zionist Archives, Jerusalem, Israel. He was a pioneer of scientific agriculture in Palestine and discoverer of wild wheat.

(Cited by Gal, *Studies in Zionism* 6:219 n. 24.)

Abbot, Edwin Hale (1834–1927). Papers: contains three letters from Brandeis, 1892–1895; also contains one letter from Brandeis to Winthrop H. Wade, 1892. Manuscript and Archives Division, Sterling Memorial Library, Yale University, New Haven, Conn. MS 61-3625. Railroad entrepreneur in Wisconsin. WWW I/1.

The bulk of the collection refers to business correspondence pertaining to Wisconsin railroad companies.

Adams, Henry Carter (1851–1921). Papers. Michigan Historical Collections, Bentley Historical Library, University of Michigan, Ann Arbor. MS 64-1402 and 81-1749. Professor of political economy at the University of Michigan, and statistician for the U.S. Interstate Commerce Commission. WWW I/7.

Alderman, Edwin Anderson (1861–1931).* Papers: contains two letters from Brandeis, 1924 and three letters from Alderman to Brandeis, 1924. University of Virginia Library, Charlottesville, Va. MS 62-2065. Educator, author, and president of the University of Virginia. WWW I/12.

Association of National Advertising Managers.** Papers: contains one letter from Brandeis, 1913. Houghton Library, Harvard University, Cambridge, Mass.

Baker, Ray Stannard (1870-1946).* Papers. Princeton University Library, Princeton, N.J. MS 72-594. Journalist, author and biographer of Woodrow Wilson. WWW II/39.

Barnard, Harry (1906-1982). Papers. Archives, American Heritage Center, University of Wyoming, Laramie. MS 84-1458. Biographer, publicist, and columnist. He wrote a biography of Judge Julian Mack, see chapter 1, *infra.* WWW VIII/22.

Baruch, Bernard Mannes (1870-1965).** Papers: contains copies of two letters from Baruch to Brandeis. Princeton University Library, Princeton, N.J. MS 71-378. Businessman, Wall Street financier and adviser to several American Presidents. WWW IV/62.

Bates, Henry Moore (1868-1949). Papers. Michigan Historical Collections, Bentley Historical Library, University of Michigan, Ann Arbor. MS 64-1430 and 81-1760. Professor of constitutional law and dean of University of Michigan Law School. WWW II/49.

Bayard, Thomas Francis (1828-1898).* Papers. Manuscript Division, Library of Congress, Washington, D.C. MS 64-764. Lawyer, U.S. Secretary of State, and Ambassador to Great Britain. WWW Hist./114.

Bedal Family Papers. ** Papers: contains two letters from Brandeis to William S. Bedal, 1935-1939. Missouri Historical Society, St. Louis, Mo.

Ben-Gurion, David (1886-1973). [See that portion of his papers relating to Zionism.] Correspondence File in American Jewish Archives, Cincinnati, Ohio. Was an ardent Zionist and prime minister of Israel, 1949-1953, and 1955-1963. WWW VI/30.

————, Papers: contains two letters from Brandeis, 1934 and 1939. Record Group Z4/15613, The Central Zionist Archives, Jerusalem, Israel.

Berger, Raoul (1901—). Papers. Harvard Law School Library, Harvard University, Cambridge, Mass. MS 84-697. Lawyer and legal scholar. Berger has written on many legal subjects including executive privilege, presidential impeachment, and judicial review. WWA 43/248.

Berlin Office of the Central Zionist Office.* Papers. Record Group Z3, The Central Zionist Archives, Jerusalem, Israel.

Billikopf, Jacob (1883-1950).* Papers. Manuscript Collection No. 13, American Jewish Archives, Cincinnati, Ohio. Was a social worker. WWW III/75.

Bogen, Boris David (1869-1929). Papers. Manuscript Collection No. 3, American Jewish Archives, Cincinnati, Ohio. MS 65-1721. Was an educator and social worker.

Bonaparte, Charles Joseph (1851–1921). Papers. Manuscript Division, Library of Congress, Washington, D.C. MS 60-2031. LC 78-13151. Lawyer, municipal and civil service reformer, and U.S. cabinet member during Woodrow Wilson's presidency. WWW I/114.

Brandeis, Fannie.* Papers. Privately held, Louisville, KY.

Brandeis, Louis Dembitz (1856–1941). Papers: ca. 1600 items and thirty-one reels of microfilm. American Jewish Archives, Cincinnati, Ohio. MS 68-1137. WWW I/131.

Consists partially of original documents and partially of copies of the Brandeis Papers that are in the Zionist Archives and Library, New York City.

———, The Public Papers of Louis Dembitz Brandeis, 1879–1916. Eight reels of microfilm. Contains 176 documents relating to Brandeis' legal concerns. Library, Brandeis University, Waltham, Mass.

There is a letter press Guide to a Microfilm Edition of "The Public Papers of Justice Louis Dembitz Brandeis in the Jacob and Bertha Goldfarb Library of Brandeis University." 1978, 57 pp., softcover. The reels are available for purchase.

———, Letters of Louis D. Brandeis. Edited by Melvin I. Urofsky and David W. Levy. 5 vols. Albany: State University of New York Press, 1971–1978.

A sixth volume is planned. See chapter 1, infra for further information.

———, Papers. The Central Zionist Archives, Jerusalem, Israel.

An extensive collection of letters written by Brandeis. The material is located in the recipient's file. Herein I have indicated the larger collections. In 1969 the Archives produced a handwritten, twenty-page inventory of its Brandeis correspondence. Unfortunately, the Archives has not updated this list.

———, Papers and Records. Zionist Archives and Library, New York, N.Y.

Contains materials on Brandeis' interest in Judaism. They have been microfilmed on 31 reels. There is a letter press index to the correspondence of Justice Louis D. Brandeis (reels 13–31 from the Zionist Archives and Library collection) produced by Deborah E. Lipstadt, Los Angeles, Calif.

———, Papers. YIVO Institute For Jewish Research, New York, N.Y.

Contains materials on Brandeis' interest in Judaism.

———, Papers: 50 feet, ca. 18,000 items. Manuscript Division, Harvard Law School Library, Harvard University, Cambridge, Mass. MS 80-1958.

Mostly Brandeis' papers compiled during his tenure (1916–1939) on the U.S. Supreme Court. There is a letter press guide entitled *Inventory of His Papers*, dated July 1, 1977. Unpaged, typescript, compiled by Erika S. Chadbourn. In 1986, University Publications of America, Inc. microfilmed this collection and is offering it for puchase in two parts. Part I, 1916–1931, 60 reels, $4,800, and Part II, 1932–1939, 34 reels, $2,700.

————, Papers: 140 feet, ca. 250,000 items. Law Library, University of Louisville, Louisville, Ky. MS 61-945.

Is divided into ten subject areas. It is the largest extant collection of Brandeis Papers. The collection was microfilmed in 1978 on 184 reels and is available for purchase at $40.00 per reel. There is a letter press *Guide to the Papers of Louis Dembitz Brandeis at the University of Louisville, Microfilm Edition.* 1979. 104 pp., softcover, which describes in detail each reel of microfilm.

————, Papers, 1926–1941, four items. Manuscript Division, Library of Congress, Washington, D.C. LC 79-282.

Broches, Samuel (1886—). Papers. American Jewish Archives, Cincinnati, Ohio. MS 67-977.

It is a collection of Zionist and American Jewish papers (records and correspondence of individuals and organizations) donated by Mr. Broches to the American Jewish Archives.

Brodie, Israel Benjamin (1884–1965).* Papers: contains forty letters from Brandeis, 1930–1941. Record Group A251/329b, Central Zionist Archives, Jerusalem, Israel. A New York City lawyer and executive of several Israeli corporations. WWW IV/120.

Burlingham, Charles Culp (1858–1959). Papers. Harvard Law School Library, Harvard University, Cambridge, Mass. MS 80-1959. New York City lawyer and civic leader. WWW III/124.

Caiserman, Hanane Meier. Papers: contains one letter from Brandeis, dated March 14, 1919, concerning the Canadian Jewish Congress. Canadian Jewish Congress Archives, Montreal, Canada.

Carnegie, Andrew (1835–1919).* Papers. Manuscript Division, Library of Congress, Washington, D.C. MS 64-767. Industrialist and philanthropist. WWW I/194.

Carson, Hampton Lawrence (1852–1929). Legal autographs. Free Library of Philadelphia, Philadelphia, Pa. MS 60-1083. Carson was a collector of legal autographs and letters written by prominent lawyers and judges. Was a Philadelphia attorney-at-law and Attorney General of Pennsylvania. WWW I/99.

Chafee, Zechariah (1885–1957).* Papers: contains thirteen letters from Brandeis, 1918–1941. Harvard Law School Library, Harvard University, Cambridge, Mass. MS 72-905. Professor of law at Harvard University. Chafee was a great exponent of freedom of speech. WW III/147.

Chandler, William Eaton (1835–1917).* Papers. New Hampshire Historical Society, Concord, N.H. MS 69-418. Lawyer, politician, and United States senator from New Hampshire. WWW I/210.

Cohen, Benjamin V. (1894–1983). Papers. Manuscript Collection No. 65, American Jewish Archives, Cincinnati, Ohio. New York City lawyer, government official and Zionist. WWW VIII/83.

The file relates to members and activities of the World Zionist Organization. The bulk of the material spans the years 1919–1921.

Cooke, Morris Llewellyn (1872–1960).* Papers. Franklin D. Roosevelt Library, Hyde Park, N.Y. MS 65-29. Scientist, consulting engineer, government official, and author. WWW III/181.

Copenhagen Office. Records of the Provisional Zionist Office at Copenhagen.* Papers: contains twenty letters from Brandeis, 1915–1916. Record Group L6/12/5 and L6/12/4, Central Zionist Archives, Jerusalem, Israel.

Cornell University. New York State School of Industrial and Labor Relations. Papers: Records of ad hoc arbitration boards, 1913–1958. New York State School of Industrial Labor Relations Collections, Cornell University, Ithaca, N.Y. MS 62-1954.
 Brandeis served as an arbitrator in the garment industry before he became a Supreme Court Justice.

De Haas, Jacob (1872–1937).* Papers. Zionist Archives and Library, New York, N.Y. He was an active American Zionist, personally knew Brandeis and wrote several articles and books on the Justice.

————, Papers. American Jewish Archives, Cincinnati, Ohio.

Contains a large file of correspondence between De Haas and Brandeis on Zionism and Palestine affairs, 1918–1936.

Denman, William (1872–1959).** Papers: contains four letters from Brandeis, 1916–1921. Bancroft Library, University of California, Berkeley, Calif. MS 75-277. Attorney and federal judge in San Francisco, Calif., was chairman of U.S. Shipping Board during World War I. WWW III/221.

Dickstein, Samuel (1885–1954). Papers. Manuscript Collection No. 8, American Jewish Archives, Cincinnati, Ohio. Was an attorney-at-law, congressman from New York, and a justice of the New York Supreme Court. WWW III/227.

The material relates to Dickstein's anti-facist (primarily anti-Nazi) activities in the United States, 1923–1944.

Dixon, Frederick (1897–1923). Papers. Manuscript Division, Library of Congress, Washington, D.C. MS 59-15. Co-founder and European editor of the *Christian Science Monitor.* WWW I/327.

Douglas Family Papers.* Papers: contains, in toto, fourteen letters from Brandeis; twelve letters are from Brandeis to James Marsh Douglas, 1937 and 1939; and twelve letters are to Walter Bond Douglas. Missouri Historical Society, St. Louis, Mo.

Ehrmann, Herbert Brutus (1891–1970).* Papers. Harvard Law School Library, Harvard University, Cambridge, Mass. MS 72-906. Boston attorney-at-law, was junior defense counsel for Nicola Sacco and Bartolomeo Vanzetti during their murder trial and appeal, 1920–1927. WWW VI/126.

Besides having letters from Brandeis, there is an article, "Louis Dembitz Brandeis" (7 pp., typed), on the Justice, which seems was never published. There is a copy of it both in the Felix Frankfurter Papers, Manuscript Division, Library of Congress, Washington, D.C., and in the Ehrmann Papers, Law Library, Harvard University, Cambridge, Mass. Ehrmann wrote the article in 1937–1938. In a covering letter to then Professor Frankfurter, he said "I have tried to make it personal but perhaps not in the desired manner."

Eliot, Charles William (1834–1926).* Papers. Archives, Library, Harvard University, Cambridge, Mass. President of Harvard University, 1869–1909. WWW I/364.

Ernst, Morris Leopold. (1888–1976).* Papers: contains seven letters from Brandeis. Library, University of Texas, Austin, Texas. An attorney-at-law in New York and author. WWW VII/182.

Ettinger, Jacob Akiba.* Papers: contains twelve letters from Brandeis, 1931–1932. Record Group A111/58, Central Zionist Archives, Jerusalem, Israel.

Evans, Elizabeth (Gardiner) (1856–1937).* Papers: contains eight letters from Brandeis, 1887–1936; plus, four folders of letters (two-inches thick) spanning 1887–1937. The bulk of this correspondence, however, is between Mrs. Evans and Mrs. Brandeis and was written in the 1930s. In Women's Archives, Arthur and Elizabeth Schlesinger Library, Radcliffe College, Cambridge, Mass. MS 61-2379. She was a close friend of Mrs. Brandeis. The correspondence reveals her concern for the Brandeis children. Mrs. Evans was a social reformer, active in the labor movement and a suffragette. WWW IV/293.

Farber, J. Eugene. Correspondence File. Contains one letter (xeroxed version) from Brandeis, dated November 7, 1920, regarding Brandeis' election to be the honorary president of Phi Epilson Rho fraternity. American Jewish Archives, Cincinnati, Ohio.

Feldman, Abraham Jehiel (1893–1977). Papers. Manuscript Collection No. 38, American Jewish Archives, Cincinnati, Ohio. MS 80-782. Reform Rabbi and civic leader of Hartford, Conn. from 1925–1968.

Fetter, Frank Albert (1863–1949).* Papers: contains ten letters from Brandeis, 1934–1941, Manuscript Division, University Libraries, University of Indiana, Bloomington, Ind. Economist, and professor of economics. WWW II/185.

Filene, Edward Albert (1860–1937).* Papers: contains five letters from Brandeis. Bergengren Memorial Museum Library, CUNA International, Inc. (Credit Union National Association) Madison, Wisc. He was a successful Boston merchant and founder of the Twentieth Century Fund. WWW I/ 396.

Fisher, Walter Lowrie (1862–1935). Papers. Manuscript Division, Library of Congress, Washington, D.C. MS 61-1509. LC 78-20669. Lawyer, municipal reformer and U.S. Secretary of the Interior, 1911–1913. WWW I/401.

Flexner, Bernard (1865–1945).* Papers. Zionist Archives and Library, New York, N.Y. Attorney-at-law in Louisville, Chicago and New York. WWW II/191.

Frankfurter, Felix (1882–1965).* Papers: (Personal). Manuscript Division, Library of Congress, Washington, D.C. MS 68-2033. LC 73-47571. Professor of law at Harvard University and, later, Associate Justice of the United States Supreme Court, 1939–1962. WWW IV/328.

Many Brandeis-Frankfurter items have disappeared from this collection.

———, Papers (his Supreme Court Papers). Harvard Law School Library, Harvard University, Cambridge, Mass. MS 72-907.

———, Papers: contains seven letters from Brandeis, 1918–1936. Record Group A 264/14, A 209/116, and Z4/1593, The Central Zionist Archives, Jerusalem, Israel.

Friedenward, Harry (1864–1950).* Papers. Record Group A 182, The Central Zionist Archives, Jerusalem, Israel. Noted Baltimore ophthalmologist, and president of the Federation of American Zionists, 1904–1918. WWW III/303.

Friendly, Henry J. (1903–1986).* Papers: a few letters from Brandeis. Personal collection. He was one of Brandeis' law clerks and a federal judge on the Second Circuit, U.S. Court of Appeals. WWA 43/1119.

Garrett, Garet (1878–1954).** Papers: contains one letter from Brandeis, 1937. Houghton Library, Harvard University, Cambridge, Mass. MS 81-509. Financial and economics writer. WWW III/314.

Glass, Carter (1858–1946).** Papers: contains one letter from Brandeis, 1919. University of Virginia Library, Charlottesville, Va. MS 60-2401. Va #2913. Farmer, newspaper publisher, political leader and U.S. senator from Virginia. WWW II/212.

Glueck, Shelton (1896–1980). Papers. Harvard Law School Library, Harvard University, Cambridge, Mass. MS 75-605. Criminologist and professor of law at Harvard Law School. WWW VII/225.

Goldenweiser, Emanuel Alexandrovich (1883–1953). Papers. Manuscript Division, Library of Congress, Washington, D.C. MS 59-27. LC 78-23010. Economist, director of the Division of Research and Statistics, Federal Reserve Board (1930–1945). WWW III/331.

Goldman, Max. Correspondence File. Contains one letter from Brandeis responding to Goldman's appeal for assistance in a Palestinian matter, December 3, 1931. American Jewish Archives, Cincinnati, Ohio.

Goldmark, Pauline. (1873–1962).* Papers. Manuscript Division, Library of Congress, Washington, D.C. LC 79-5248. Was a welfare worker and a reformer. WWW IV/365 and V/275.

Gottheil, Richard James Horatio (1862–1936).* Papers: contains fifty-four letters from Brandeis, 1914–1919. Record Group A 138/9, The Central Zionist Archives, Jerusalem, Israel. Professor of semetic languages and an editor of the *Jewish Encyclopedia*. WWW I/473.

————, Papers. Manuscript Collection No. 127, American Jewish Archives, Cincinnati, Ohio.

In one letter, dated November 20, 1934, Brandeis thanked Gottheil for a birthday greeting.

Grady, Alice Harriet (1873–1934).* Papers: contains ninety-nine letters from Brandeis. Goldfarb Library, Brandeis University, Waltham, Mass. Was Brandeis' private secretary when he practiced law in Boston.

————, "A Collection of 114 autograph letters and notes in the hand of Justice Brandeis, with substantial additional material. (Washington, D.C. and other locations) 1917–1929."

This collection is being offered for sale by Meyer Boswell Books, 982 Hayes Street, San Francisco, Cal. 94117.

Gratz Family Collection.** Papers: contains three Brandeis letters, to Mr. Roule (1900) and to Mrs. Gratz (1924). Historical Society of Pennsylvania, Philadelphia, Pa. MS 60-2336. This Philadelphia family dates back to the eighteenth century.

Gray, John Chipman (1839-1915).* Papers: contains two letters from Brandeis, 189?-191?. Houghton Library, Harvard University, Cambridge, Mass. Lawyer and professor of law at Harvard Law School. WWW I/479.

Greene, Evarts Boutell (1870-1947). Papers: contains one letter from Brandeis, 1931. Special Collections, Columbia University Libraries. New York, N.Y. MS 78-687. Professor of history at the University of Illinois and at Columbia University. WWW II/221.

Gressman, Eugene (1917—). Papers. Michigan Historical Collections, Bentley Historical Library, University of Michigan, Ann Arbor. MS 80-1236. Attorney-at-law in Washington, D.C. He was a law clerk to U.S. Supreme Court Justice Frank Murphy. WWA 43/1295.

Haines, Lynn (1876-1929). Papers. Minnesota Historical Society Collections, St. Paul, Minn. MS 60-1374. Publicist and journalist. Includes materials assembled by Haines while he was editor of *Searchlight on Congress,* a publication of the National Voters League.

Hale, Robert Lee (1884-1969). Papers: contains seven letters from Brandeis, 1922-1939. Special Collections, Columbia University Libraries, New York, N.Y. MS 78-689. Professor of law at Columbia University. WWW V/297.

Hand, Learned (1872-1961).* Papers: contains fourteen letters from Brandeis, 1916-1937. Harvard Law School Library, Harvard University, Cambridge, Mass. MS 72-908. Judge, United States Court of Appeals, Second Circuit. WWW IV/401-402.

Handler, Milton (1903—). Papers: contains eight letters from Brandeis, 1928-1933. Special Collections, Columbia University Law Library, New York, N.Y. MS 80-1908. Attorney and professor of law at Columbia University. He was a law clerk to United States Supreme Court Justice Harlan Fiske Stone. WWA 43/1369.

Hapgood, Norman (1868-11937).** Papers: contains one letter from Brandeis, 1913. Manuscript and Archives Division, Sterling Memorial Library, Yale University, New Haven, Conn. Editor and author. WWW I/517.

Heller, James Gutheim (1892-1971). Papers. Manuscript Collection No. 147, American Jewish Archives, Cincinnati, Ohio. Reform Rabbi in Cincinnati, Ohio, and composer of religious music. WWW V/323.

Heller, Maximalian (1860-1929). Papers. Manuscript Collection No. 33, American Jewish Archives, Cincinnati, Ohio. MS 67-1004. Reform Rabbi in Chicago and New Orleans. WWW I/547.

Hoffman, Edward J. Papers: contains one letter from Brandeis, 1937. American Jewish Archives, Cincinnati, Ohio.

In the letter, dated November 17, 1937, Brandeis granted permission to name a B'nai B'rith Lodge in Malden, Mass. after him.

Holmes, Oliver Wendell (1841-1935).* Papers: contains forty-three letters from Brandeis, 1891-1934. Harvard Law School Library, Harvard University, Cambridge, Mass. MS 72-909. Associate Justice of the United States Supreme Court, 1902-1932. WWW I/582.

Horner, Henry (1878-1940).** Papers: contains two letters from Brandeis. Illinois State Historical Library, Springfield, Ill. Lawyer and was governor of Illinois, 1933-1941. WWW I/588.

One letter from Brandeis, dated November 19, 1934, acknowledging Horner's birthday greetings and one telegram, dated November 13, 1935, is from Horner to Brandeis conveying his birthday wishes.

Houghton, Henry Oscar (1823-1895).** Papers: contains four letters from Brandeis, 1891, 1893. Houghton Library, Harvard University, Cambridge, Mass. MS 82-627. Was a book publisher, and founder of Houghton, Mifflin and Company. WWW Hist./331.

House, Edward Mandell (1858-1938).* Papers: contains eleven letters from Brandeis, 1914-1919. Manuscript and Archives Division, Sterling Memorial Library, Yale University, New Haven, Conn. MS 61-3488. Adviser to President Woodrow Wilson. WWW I/592.

Howe, Mark Antony deWolf (1906-1967).* Papers. Harvard Law School Library, Harvard University, Cambridge, Mass. MS 76-1910. Professor of law at University of Buffalo Law School and at Harvard Law School. WWW IV/466.

Hudson, Manley Ottmer (1886-1960). Papers. Harvard Law School Library, Harvard University, Cambridge, Mass. MS 72-910. Professor of law at the University of Missouri and at Harvard Law School, and a mediator and judge of international law disputes. WWW IV/470.

Huebsch, Benjamin W. (1876-1964).* Papers. Manuscript Division, Library of Congress, Washington, D.C. MS 66-1421. Was a book publisher. WWW IV/471.

Hurwitz, Henry (1886-1961).* Papers. Manuscript Collection No. 2, American Jewish Archives, Cincinnati, Ohio. Educator and founded the periodical *The Menorah Journal.* WWW IV/477.

Industrial Removal Office. Records. American Jewish Historical Society, Waltham, Mass. MS 72-1372.

Correspondence, minutes, reports, etc., of a non-profit organization that attempted to move immigrants out of the congested tenements of New York City and settle them in cities and towns throughout the United States.

Kallen, Horace Meyer (1882–1974). Papers. YIVO Institute for Jewish Research Library, New York, N.Y. MS 60-2600. Educator, writer, and philosopher. He wrote several articles and books on Brandeis. WWW VI/219.

————, Papers. Manuscript Collection No. 1 and Rare Documents File, American Jewish Archives, Cincinnati, Ohio. MS 65-1728 and 80-790.

Kelley, Nicholas (1885–1965). Papers. New York Public Library, New York, N.Y. MS 74-532. Attorney-at-law in New York City. Was associated with many civic, humanitarian, cultural and legal organizations. WWW IV/517.

Kellogg, Paul Underwood (1879–1958). Papers: contains fifteen letters, mostly between Kellogg and Brandeis. Social Welfare History Archives, University of Minnesota Library, Minneapolis, Minn. MS 70-1652. Journalist, social reformer, and editor of *The Survey* 1912–1942. WWW III/467.

————, Papers: contains thirty-five letters from Brandeis to Paul Underwood Kellogg; plus nineteen to Paul Kellogg, and one to Arthur P. Kellogg (Paul's brother). Goldfarb Library, Brandeis University, Waltham, Mass.

Kent, William (1864–1928).** Papers: contains two letters from Brandeis, 1912 and 1913. Manuscript and Archives Division, Sterling Memorial Library, Yale University, New Haven, Conn. MS 62-3510. U.S. representative from California. Was interested in progressive conservation programs. WWW I/669.

Kessleman, Robert D.* Papers: contains forty-one letters from Brandeis, 1922–1939. Record Group A 168/7 and A 251/329b. The Central Zionist Archives, Jerusalem, Israel.

Kingsbury, John Adams (1876–1956). Papers. Manuscript Division, Library of Congress, Washington, D.C. MS 64-1572. LC 73-28662. New York City social worker. WWW III/479.

Kirsh, Benjamin Sollow (1898—).* Papers. Privately held, New York, N.Y. A New York City attorney. Was a law partner with Samuel Rosenman and Brandeis' daughter, Susan.

Kohler, Max J. (1871–1934).** Papers: contains ten letters from Brandeis. American Jewish Historical Society, Waltham, Mass. MS 68-143. New York City attorney and was active in Jewish community matters. WWW I/690.

La Follette, Philip Fox (1897–1965). Papers. The State Historical Society of Wisconsin, Madison. MS 62-2647. Was governor of the State of Wisconsin, and a leader of the Progressive Party. WWW IV/549.

La Follette Family Collection.* Papers: includes letters from Louis D. and Alice G. Brandeis. Manuscript Division, Library of Congress, Washington, D.C. MS 82-1203. LC 79-29165.

Includes papers of Robert M. La Follette, Sr. (1855–1925), Robert M. La Follette, Jr. (1918–1953) and several other members of the family. The Robert La Follettes Sr. & Jr. were U.S. senators from Wisconsin and leaders in the Progressive era.

Landis, James McCauley (1899–1964). Papers. Manuscript Division, Library of Congress, Washington, D.C. MS 68-2047. LC 78-29348. Was one of Brandeis' law clerks, professor of law and dean of the Harvard Law School, administrative law authority, and held several high positions in the federal government. WWW IV/552.

Laski, Harold Joseph. (1893–1950). Papers. Syracuse University Library, Syracuse, New York. MS 68-1734. British political scientist, author, and historian.

————, Papers. Yale Law Library, Yale University, New Haven, Conn.

Lassiter, Francis Rives (1866–1909).** Papers: contains one letter from Brandeis, 1887. Duke University Library, Durham, N.C. Attorney. Was a U.S. representative from Virginia. WWW I/706.

Lazaron, Morris S. (1888–d.). Papers: contains several letters from Brandeis, 1925–1936. Manuscript Collection No. 71, American Jewish Archives, Cincinnati, Ohio. Was a Reform Rabbi in Baltimore, Maryland and an author. WWW VIII/239.

Lehman, Herbert Henry (1878–1963).* Papers: contains two letters from Brandeis and thirteen replies. Herbert Lehman Suite, School of International Affairs, Columbia University, New York, N.Y. MS 70-129. Governor and U.S. senator from New York. WWW IV/565-566.

Levinthal, Louis Edward (1892–1976).* Papers. Privately held, Philadelphia, Pa. Philadelphia attorney and active in many Jewish organizations. WWW VII/347.

Lloyd, Henry Demarest (1847–1903).* Papers. The State Historical Society of Wisconsin, Madison, Wisc. MS 62-3521. Journalist and author. WWW I/737.

Lodge, Henry Cabot, Sr. (1850–1924).** Papers: contains several Brandeis letters. Massachusetts Historical Society, Boston, Mass. [MS number has not yet been assigned.] U.S. senator from Massachusetts. WWW I/740.

McAdoo, William Gibbs (1863–1941).* Papers. Manuscript Division, Library of Congress, Washington, D.C. MS 59-229. Lawyer, business executive, Democratic Party leader, and U.S. Secretary of the Treasury. WWW I/795.

McCarthy, Charles (1873–1921).* Papers. The State Historical Society of Wisconsin, Madison, Wisc. MS 62-2672. Political scientist, publicist and first Wisconsin legislative reference librarian. WWW I/798.

Mack, Julian William (1866–1943).* Papers. Zionist Archives and Library, New York, N.Y. Served as a judge on the United States Court of Appeals, and was a leader in the American Zionist movement. WWW II/337.

————, Papers. American Jewish Archives, Cincinnati, Ohio.

————, Papers: contains twenty-four letters from Brandeis, 1930–1934. Record Group A 251/329a and A 251/329b, The Central Zionist Archives, Jerusalem, Israel.

McReynolds, James Clark (1862–1946).* Papers: contains one letter from Brandeis. University of Virginia Law Library, Charlottesville, Va. MS 64-798. U.S. Supreme Court Justice, 1914–1941. WWW II/365.

McSwain, John Jackson (1875–1936).** Papers: contains two letters from Brandeis, 1933 and 1936. Duke University Library, Durham, N.C. MS 61-3682. Lawyer, army officer during World War I and U.S. representative from South Carolina. WWW I/824.

Magnes, Judah Leon (1877–1948).* Papers: contains five letters from Brandeis, 1915. Record Groups L 6/42, L 6/54, S 25/237 and Z 3/90 in The Central Zionist Archives, Jerusalem, Israel. Reform Rabbi in New York City, and president of Hebrew University, Jerusalem, Israel. WWW II/340–341.

Marcus, Jacob Rader (1896—). Papers: contains three letter from Brandeis, 1929–1937. American Jewish Archives, Cincinnati, Ohio. MS 68-1142. Is a professor of Jewish history, and director of the American Jewish Archives. WWA 43/2099.

Marshall, Louis (1856–1929).* Papers. American Jewish Archives, Cincinnati, Ohio. MS 65-1729. New York lawyer and philanthropist. WWW I/780.

Middleton, George (1880–1967).* Papers. Manuscript Division, Library of Congress, Washington, D.C. MS 70-962. LC 78-32839. Author, playwright and copyright law specialist. WWW IV/658.

Mitchell, John (1870–1919).* Papers: contains three letters from Brandeis. Catholic University of America Library, Washington, D.C. MS 61-1396. Labor union official. WWW I/850.

Moore, William Underhill (1879–1949).* Papers: contains one letter from Brandeis, 1919. Special Collections, Columbia University Libraries, New York, N.Y. MS 61-3346. Professor of law at Columbia University. WWW II/380.

Morgan, Arthur Ernest (1878–1975).** Papers: contains three letters from Brandeis. Houghton Library, Harvard University, Cambridge, Mass. MS 81-610. Civil engineer and educator. WWW VI/292.

Morgenthau, Henry Sr. (1856–1946).* Papers. Manuscript Division, Library of Congress, Washington, D.C. MS 60-124. Businessman and diplomat. Ambassador to Turkey. WWW II/383.

Motzkin, Leo.* Papers: contains eight letters from Brandeis, 1915. Record Group A 126/41/7 and L 6/12/1, The Central Zionist Archives, Jerusalem, Israel.

Murdock, Victor (1871–1945).* Papers. Manuscript Division, Library of Congress, Washington, D.C. MS 71-1386. U.S. representative from Kansas and newspaper editor in Wichita, Kansas. WWW II/390.

National Association of Jewish Social Workers. Records. American Jewish Historical Society, Waltham, Mass. MS 72-1380.

Correspondence, programs, and other records of said organization.

Newlands, Francis Griffith (1848–1917).** Papers: contains one letter from Brandeis, 1912. Manuscript and Archives Division, Sterling Memorial Library, Yale University, New Haven, Conn. MS 68-883. U.S. senator from Nevada. WWW I/893–894.

Newman, Louis Israel (1893–1972). Papers: several letters from Brandeis. Personal collection. Was a Rabbi in New York City, an author, and a leader in the American Zionist movement. In the 1930s, he was closely associated with the Revisionist Movement. WWW V/531.

Newmann, Emanuel.* Papers. Privately held. New York, N.Y.

Nutter, McClennan and Fish, Esq. (Boston, Mass.) Papers. Archives, Ekstrom Library, University of Louisville, Louisville, Ky.

Brandeis was associated with this law firm until he joined the United States Supreme Court in 1916.

Thornton Oakley Collection. Contemporary Club, Philadelphia, Pa. Papers: Historical Society of Pennsylvania, Philadelphia, Pa. MS 72-1184.

Papers and publications of a public affairs discussion group collected by Mr. Oakley while he served as an officer of said club.

Palestine Office. Records of the Palestina Amt at Jaffa.* Papers. Record Group L 2, The Central Zionist Archives, Jerusalem, Israel.

Palmer, Paul A. (1900—).* Papers: contains two letters from Brandeis, 1939 and 1940. Manuscript and Archives Division, Sterling Memorial Library, Yale University, New Haven, Conn. MS 62-3286. Journalist and editor.

Phelan, James Duval (1861–1930).** Papers: contains two letters from Brandeis, 1923 and 1930. Bancroft Library, University of California, Berkeley, Calif. MS 75-353. U.S. senator from California. WWW I/966.

Pilchik, Ely E. Correspondence file. Contains one letter, dated October 7, 1974, from Rabbi Pilchik (Short Hills, N.J.), concerning Professor Nathanson's article on Brandeis. See chap. 5, *infra.* American Jewish Congress, Cincinnati, Ohio.

Pinchot, Amos Richards Eno. (1873–11944).* Papers. Manuscript Division, Library of Congress, Washington, D.C. MS 59-142. LC 78-36251. Lawyer, social activist, and reformer. WWW II/425.

Pinchot, Gifford (1865–1946).* Papers. Manuscript Division, Library of Congress, Washington, D.C. MS 59-50. LC 78-36277. Forester, college professor, governor of Pennsylvania, and author. WWW II/425.

Pound, Roscoe (1870–1964).* Papers: contains twenty-three letters from Brandeis, 1909–1919. Harvard Law School Library, Harvard University, Cambridge, Mass. MS 72-911. Botanist, lawyer, professor of law, and dean of Harvard Law School. One of the great legal thinkers of the twentieth century. WWW IV/762.

Powell, Thomas Reed (1880–1955).* Papers: contains five letters from Brandeis, 1923–1938. Harvard Law School Library, Harvard University, Cambridge, Mass. MS 74-334. Professor of law at Harvard Law School. WWW III/697.

Raushenbush, Elizabeth Brandeis. Papers. Personal collection, Madison, Wisc. She is the younger daughter of the Justice.

Reading, Earl of (1860–196?).** (Rufus Daniel Isaacs). Papers: contains one letter from Brandeis introducing Lincoln Steffens to the Earl, 1922. Special Collections, Columbia University Libraries, New York, N.Y. WWW IV/779.

Redfield, William Cox (1858–1932).* Papers. Manuscript Division, Library of Congress, Washington, D.C. LC 82-37432. Was U.S. Secretary of Commerce under President Wilson. WWW I/1015.

Richards, Bernard Gerson (1877–d.).* Papers: extensive amount of Brandeis letters. Personal collection. Founder of American Jewish Congress, and was chairman of the Jewish Information Bureau. WWW V/604.

Richberg, Donald Randall (1881–1960).* Papers. Chicago Historical Society, Chicago, Illinois. MS 69-105. Lawyer in Chicago until 1933, and author. Was general counsel of the National Recovery Administration and executive director of the National Emergency Council during the New Deal years. WWW IV/791.

————, * Papers. Manuscript Division, Library of Congress, Washington, D.C. MS 59-10.

These papers are primarily concerned with the New Deal Era.

Roosevelt, Franklin Delano (1882-1945).* Papers: contains nine letters from Brandeis. Franklin D. Roosevelt Library, Hyde Park, N.Y. MS 75-562. Thirty-first President of the United States. Roosevelt's personal file contains letters, memoranda, telegrams, etc. concerning Brandeis, mainly written around 1936. WWW II/457.

Roper, Daniel Calhoun. (1867-1943).** Papers: contains one letter from Brandeis, 1932. Duke University Library, Durham, N.C. Attorney, U.S. senator from North Carolina, and held two cabinet positions. WWW II/458.

Rosenblatt, Bernard.** Papers: contains four notes from Brandeis, 1912-1916. Personal collection. New York City attorney and was involved in the American Zionist movement.

Rosenthal, Albert (1863-1939).* Papers: contains one letter from Brandeis (1932) acknowledging receipt of a copy of his portrait. Historical Society of Pennsylvania, Philadelphia, Pa. Artist and portrait painter. WWW I/1058.

————, Papers. Archives of American Art, Detroit, Mich. MS 67-1130.

Rubenstein, Frank J. Correspondence file. Contains one letter from Brandeis dated January 13, 1932. American Jewish Archives, Cincinnati, Ohio.

Saffro, Joseph (1878-1959). Papers. Wisconsin Jewish Archives, The State Historical Society of Wisconsin, Madison. MS 68-2322. Zionist.

Includes correspondence and financial papers pertaining to Zionist activities in Milwaukee, Wisc. and Brandeis' visit in 1914 to that city.

Savings Bank Life Insurance. Woburn, Mass.* Papers: contains numerous letters from Brandeis. To keep himself abreast of the movement he started, Brandeis requested correspondence from their files be sent to him.

Schiff, Jacob Henry (1847-1920).* Papers. American Jewish Archives, Cincinnati, Ohio. MS 65-1739. Financier and philanthropist. WWW I/1087.

Scott, Austin Wakeman (1884-1981). Papers: Harvard Law School Library, Harvard University, Cambridge, Mass. MS 84-703. Was an expert on the law of trusts and civil procedure, and a professor of law at Harvard Law School. WWW III/511.

Seligman, Edwin Robert Anderson (1861–1939).* Papers: contains four letters from Brandeis, 1911–1929. Special Collections, Columbia University Libraries. New York, N.Y. MS 62-556. Economist, and professor of economics. WWW I/1102-1103.

Silver, Abba Hillel (1893–1963).* Papers. Archives of Temple Tifereth Israel, University Circle at Silver Park, Cleveland, Ohio, 44106. Rabbi in Cleveland, Ohio. WWW IV/863-864.

Sinclair, Upton Beall (1878–1968).** Papers: contains five letters from Brandeis, 1927–1933. Manuscript Division, University Libraries, Indiana University, Bloomington, Ind.

Political activist and author who is most renowned for his novels advocating social reform, e.g., *The Jungle.*

Sokolow, Nahum.* Papers: contains six letters from Brandeis, 1913–1918. Record Group Z 4/1593 and Z 3/404. The Central Zionist Archives, Jerusalem, Israel.

Society of Jewish Social Workers, New York. Records. American Jewish Historical Society, Waltham, Mass. MS 72-1388.

Correspondence, minutes of said organization.

Speed, Hattie Bishop.* Papers. J. B. Speed Museum, Louisville, Ky.

Stanley, Augustus Owsley (1867–1958).** Papers: contains one letter from Brandeis, 1914. Edward M. House Papers, Manuscript and Archives Divison, Sterling Memorial Library, Yale University, New Haven, Conn. Attorney-at-law and U.S. senator from Kentucky, 1919–1925. WWW III/812.

Steffens, (Joseph) Lincoln (1866–1936).* Papers: one letter from Brandeis to Mr. Steffens (1909) and one letter to Mrs. Steffens (1937). Special Collections, Columbia University Libraries, New York, N.Y. MS 61-3444. Journalist, social and economic reformer. WWW I/1176.

Stimson, Henry Lewis (1867–1950). Papers: contains six letters from Brandeis, (1910–1941) and one from Mrs. Brandeis (1941). Manuscript and Archives Division, Sterling Memorial Library, Yale University, New Haven, Conn. MS 61-3472. U.S. Secretary of War, 1911–1913 and 1940-1945. WWW III/822.

Superior Court of the Pow Wow, Harvard Law School, Pow Wow Briefs, 1871–1885, 375 items. Harvard Law School Library, Harvard University, Cambridge, Mass. MS 80-1971.

Legal briefs of plantiffs and defendants in cases argued in the court, a student club at Harvard Law School. "Includes briefs of law students . . . Louis D. Brandeis."

Sutherland, George (1862–1942). Papers. Manuscript Divison, Library of Congress, Washington, D.C. MS 60-3221. LC 78-42002. Lawyer, senator from Utah, and associate justice of United States Supreme Court, 1922–1938. WWW II/519.

Szold, Henrietta (1860–1945).* Papers: (private) contains fifteen letters from Brandeis, 1927–1941. Record Group A 125/55, The Central Zionist Archives, Jerusalem, Israel. Founder of Hadassah and ardent Zionist. WWW II/522.

Szold, Robert (1889–1977).* Papers: The amount of Brandeis correspondence is vast, 1930–1941. Zionist Archives and Library, New York, N.Y. Was a New York City attorney and was active in the American Zionist movement. Was chairman of the board of the Palestine Economic Corporation, 1945–1960. WWW VII/560.

————, Papers: contains forty letters from Brandeis, 1930–1938. Record Group A 251/329a and A 251/329b, The Central Zionist Archives, Jerusalem, Israel.

Tachau, Jean Brandeis. *Memoirs of Jean Brandeis Tachau (August 22, 1894– July 3, 1978).* 71 pp. typescript. Archives, Eskstrom Library, University of Louisville, Louisville, Ky. She was the daughter of Alfred Brandeis, Louis' older brother.

See especially pp. 62–71, which contain correspondence between Allon Gal and Tachau regarding the relationship between Alfred and Louis. [While this is a book, I put the entry here because of its limited distribution.]

Taft, William Howard (1857–1930).* Papers. Manuscript Division, Library of Congress, Washington, D.C. MS 62-4597. Was twenty-seventh President of the United States, and Chief Justice of the United States Supreme Court, 1921–1930. WWW I/1213.

Tannenbaum, Frank (1893–1969).* Papers: contains four letters from Brandeis, 1929–1931. Special Collections, Columbia University Libraries, New York, N.Y. MS 61-3443, and 73-105. Director of University Seminars and professor of Latin American history at Columbia University.

Teal, Joseph Nathan (1858–1929). Papers. Oregon Historical Society Library, Portland, Ore. MS 76-1236. Rancher, lawyer, and public official of Portland, Oregon. WWW I/1222.

Thayer, Ezra Ripley (1866–1915). Papers. Harvard Law School Library, Harvard University, Cambridge, Mass. MS 76-1923. Professor of law and dean of Harvard Law School. WWW I/1226.

Thomas, Alsen Franklin (1862-?). Papers. University of Virginia Library, Charlottesville, Va. MS 74-1139. Author and state legislator.

Thompson, Huston (1875-1966).* Papers. Manuscript Division, Library of Congress, Washington, D.C. MS 67-633. Lawyer and government official. Was a mediator of several national industrial strikes (1934-1952). WWW IV/938.

Tucker, Henry St. George (1853-1932).** Papers. Southern Historical Collection, Library, University of North Carolina, Chapel Hill, N.C. Was a U.S. congressman from Virginia, and professor of law. WWW I/1256.

> While not containing any letters from Brandeis, has two items written by Tucker in 1916 which voice strong opposition to Brandeis' nomination to the Supreme Court.

United States Department of State.* Records Relating to Palestine. Record Group 59, The National Archives, Washington, D.C.

United States Railroad Securities Commission.* Records: 1890-1914, contains twelve letters from Brandeis. Manuscript and Archives Division, Sterling Memorial Library, Yale University, New Haven, Conn. MS 68-1444.

> Is the records of said organization.

Van Devanter, Willis (1859-1941).* Papers. Manuscript Division, Library of Congress, Washington, D.C. LC 82-43,950. Was an Associate Justice of the U.S. Supreme Court, 1910-1937. WWW I/1269.

Villard, Oswald Garrison (1872-1949).** Papers: contains four letters from Brandeis, 1930-1941. Houghton Library, Harvard University, Cambridge, Mass. MS 70-516. Author and journalist. Was co-founder of the N.A.A.C.P. WWW II/548.

Wald, Lillian D. (1867-1940).* Papers: contains two letters from Brandeis, 1911 and 1915. Special Collections, Columbia University Libraries, New York, N.Y. MS 69-645. Social worker and reformer, founder of the Henry Street (N.Y.) Settlement. WWW I/1287.

Warren, Charles (1868-1954).* Papers. Manuscript Division, Library of Congress, Washington, D.C. MS 67-635. Boston lawyer and legal historian. WWW III/891.

Wehle, Louis Brandeis (1880-1959).* Papers. Franklin D. Roosevelt Library, Hyde Park, N.Y. MS 65-79. Was an attorney in Louisville, Ky. and in New York City, and federal government official. WWW III/899.

Weinberger, Harry (1886-1944).* Papers: contains nine letters from Brandeis, 1917-1925. Manuscript and Archives Division, Sterling Memorial Library, Yale University, New Haven, Conn. MS 74-1207. Attorney in New York

City. Worked on behalf of the legal rights of radicals, anarchists, aliens and immigrants.

Weizmann, Chaim (1874-1952).* Papers. Library of Yad Chaim Weizmann, Rehovot, Israel. Chemist, was instrumental in the creation of the Balfour Declaration, and first president of the State of Israel. WWW IV/994.

————, Papers: contains sixteen letters from Brandeis, 1914-1918. Record Group Z4/1593 and Z3/758. The Central Zionist Archives, Jerusalem, Israel.

White, William Allen (1868-1944).* Papers. Manuscript Division, Library of Congress, Washington, D.C. MS 59-41. Author and editor of *The Emporia (Kansas) Gazette.* Commentator on American social and public matters. WWW II/573.

Whitlock, Brand (1869-1934).* Papers. Manuscript Division, Library of Congress, Washington, D.C. MS 59-43. Lawyer, author, mayor of Toledo, Ohio (1905-1912), and ambassador to Belgium (1913-1922). WWW I/1338-1339.

Wieck, Edward A. (1884-ca. 1955). Papers. Labor History Archives, Wayne State University, Detroit, Michigan. MS 66-1528. Was a coal miner in Illinois, local official of the United Mine Workers of America, and a research assistant for the Russell Sage Foundation of New York City.

Wilson, Woodrow (1856-1924).* Papers. Manuscript Division, Library of Congress, Washington, D.C. MS. 72-1779. LC 73-46029. Was twenty-eighth President of the United States. He appointed Brandeis to the United States Supreme Court in 1916. WWW I/1364.

Wingate, Charles Edgar Lewis (1861-1944).* Papers: contains one letter from Brandeis, 1886. Houghton Library, Harvard University, Cambridge, Mass. Was a newspaperman and editor of the *Boston Sunday Post.* WWW II/586.

Wise, Stephen Samuel (1874-1949).* Papers. American Jewish Archives, Cincinnati, Ohio. MS 68-1154. Rabbi and teacher in New York City and Jewish leader. Was one of the leading Jewish personalities of this century. WWW II/587.

————, Papers. American Jewish Historical Society, Waltham, Mass. MS 77-50.

Wohl, Samuel. Papers. Manuscript Collection No. 106 and Rare Documents file, American Jewish Archives, Cincinnati, Ohio.

Woolley, Robert Wickliffe (1871-1958).* Papers. Manuscript Division, Library of Congress, Washington, D.C. MS 61-2532. LC 78-46409. Democratic Party publicity leader, journalist, and public official. WWW III/940.

World Zionist Organization.* Records of the Political Department. Papers. Record Group S 24, The Central Zionist Archives, Jerusalem, Israel.

World Zionist Organization/Jewish Agency for Palestine, London Office.* Papers. Record Group Z 4, The Central Zionist Archives, Jerusalem, Israel.

Zieve, Moshe Menachem. Papers. Correspondence Box 698, American Jewish Archives, Cincinnati, Ohio.

Contains correspondence and documents concerning the development of the British mandate in Palestine and related Zionist activity, 1917–1921.

CHAPTER 7

Speeches Given by Justice Brandeis

Besides speeches, this chapter includes interviews and various miscellaneous written statements. Not every Brandeis speech was transcribed. There does not seem to be any permanent recording of Justice Brandeis delivering a speech. The Jewish Museum's National Jewish Archive of Broadcasting in New York City never answered my two queries on this issue.

This listing does not include oral presentations that Brandeis made either in courts or before governmental entities (i.e., hearings). For this information, consult Professor Mersky's bibliography.

This chapter is based on several earlier compiled sources, namely:

Drushal, *The Speeches of Louis Dembitz Brandeis, 1908–1916.* (1951), pp. 524–526 which list speeches only to 1916. Cited herein as Drushal;

Harris, *Zionist Speeches of Louis Dembitz Brandeis; A Critical Edition.* (1968), pp. 479–480, herein cited as Harris;

Mersky. *Louis Dembitz Brandeis, 1856–1941, A Bibliography.* (1958), pp. 19–27, herein cited as Mersky;

Urofsky and Levy, editors. *Letters of Louis D. Brandeis*, 5 vols. (1971–1978), cited herein as U&L;

A typed two-page bibliography entitled *Bibliography of Brandeisiana on Zionism* (unsigned and undated) that I found in the vertical file of the Zionist Archives and Library in New York City, cited herein as ZAL.

This chapter also incorporates my own research. Among other sources, I went through the six major sources listed below that print Brandeis' speeches and articles:

Brandeis, Louis D. *Brandeis on Zionism: A Collection of Addresses and Statements by Louis D. Brandeis.* . . . Washington, D.C.: Zionist Organization of America, 1942. Cited herein as *Brandeis on Zionism.*

Brandeis, Louis D. *Business—A Profession.* Boston: Small, Maynard & Company, 1914. There have been later editions. The pagination varies from edition to edition. Cited herein as *Business—A Profession.*

Brandeis, Louis D. *The Curse of Bigness: Miscellaneous Papers of Louis D. Brandeis.* Edited by Osmond K. Fraenkel. Port Washington, N.Y.: Kennikat Press, Inc., 1934. Cited herein as *Curse of Bigness.*

Brandeis, Louis D. *The Social and Economic Views of Mr. Justice Brandeis.* Collected with Introductory Notes, by Alfred Lief. New York: Vanguard Press, 1930. Cited herein as *Social and Economic Views.*

This volume mainly contains reprints of Brandeis' Supreme Court decisions. However, pp. 337–415 (Part VII) entitled "Ideas Expressed Before 1916" excerpts speeches and articles made by Brandeis before he joined the High Court.

Brandeis University. Library. *Guide to a Microfilm Edition of the Public Papers of Justice Louis Dembitz Brandeis in the Jacob and Bertha Goldfarb Library of Brandeis University.* (1978). Cited herein as Brandeis Univ. Document(s).

One hundred seventy-six documents (articles, speeches, briefs of Brandeis) were put on eight reels of microfilm and are offered for sale.

De Haas, Jacob. *Louis D. Brandeis—A Biographical Sketch . . . With Full Text of His Addresses Delivered from 1912 to 1924.* New York: Bloch Publishing Company, 1929. Cited herein as De Haas. The speeches are printed at pp. 151–296, and,

Lastly, my own research in the Brandeis Papers at the University of Louisville Law Library, cited herein as Brandeis Papers.

1897, October 27.

"A More Beautiful Life." Brandeis and Professor Albert H. Munsell spoke before the Young Men's Congregational Club at the American House, Boston. Source: Brandeis Papers, Box 233. p. 146.

1901, June 19.

"Louis D. Brandeis Reviews Recent Subway History." An interview printed in the *Boston Evening Transcript,* June 19, 1901. Reprinted in Brandeis Univ. Document 16.

1902, December 4.

"The Incorporation of Trades Unions." Given as part of a "debate" with Samuel Gompers, president of the American Federation of Labor at the

Economic Club of Boston at the Tremont Temple. Brandeis' speech was printed in the *Boston Post,* December 5, 1902; *Boston Herald,* December 5, 1902; and *The Green Bag* 15:11-14 (January 1903). Reprinted in *Business—A Profession,* 82-98; and Brandeis Univ. Documents 50 and 51. Listed by Mersky; and U&L I:232-233.

Brandeis redelivered this speech at the American Social Science Association on May 14, 1903.

1903, February 25.

Untitled. Brandeis read a paper on the subject of municipal ownership and public franchises at the National Convention on Municipal Ownership and Public Franchises at the Reform Club, New York City. After much revision it was printed as the "The Experience of Massachusetts in Street Railways." *Municipal Affairs* 6:721-729 (Winter 1902-03). Listed by U&L I:220. Source: Brandeis Papers, Box 233, pp. 244-245.

1903, March 18.

Untitled. Address on municipal corruption delivered before the Boot and Shoe Club, Hotel Brunswick, Boston. Was printed in the *Boston Post,* March 19, 1903, p. 1; the *Boston Herald,* and the *Boston Evening Transcript* of the same date. Reprinted in *Curse of Business,* 263-265, as "Address on Corruption"; and Brandeis Univ. Document 26. Listed by Mersky; and U&L I:226.

1903, April 8.

"Searchlight Needed on City Hall." An address given at the monthly meeting of the Unitarian Club, at the Hotel Vendome, Boston. Reported in the *Boston Post, Boston Herald,* and *Boston Globe,* all on April 9, 1903. Source: Brandeis Papers, Box 233, File 5, p. 157.

The topic of his speech was misrepresentation of Boston city government.

1903, May 14.

"The Incorporation of Trade Unions." See December 4, 1902 entry.

1903, December 11.

Untitled. An address that "summarizes Brandeis' view on the futility of relying on the rhetoric instead of political action to attack civic abuse." Delivered before the Good Government Association, Boston. Reprinted in Brandeis Univ. Documents 21 and 27. A typed version of the speech is in the Brandeis Papers, Box 233, pp. 167-169.

1904, March 30.

"Compensation for the Use of Streets." Delivered before the Good Government League, Cambridge, Mass. Printed in the *Cambridge Chronicle,* 17-18, April 9, 1904. Reprinted in Brandeis Univ. Document 22. Listed by Mersky.

1904, April 21.

"The Employer and Trades Unions." Delivered before the annual meeting of the Boston Typothetae, Somerset Hotel, Boston. Reported in the *Boston Herald*, April 22, 1904. Printed in *National Civic Federation Monthly Review* 1:10-11 (August 1904); and as a pamphlet, 18 pp. Reprinted in *Business—A Profession*, 13-27; and Brandeis Univ. Document 53. Listed by Mersky; and U&L I:246-247.

Brandeis was the counsel of the Boston Typothetae, an association of employers, during a memorable struggle with the typographical union.

1904, November 16.

"Labor's Monopoly vs. That of Capital." Brandeis spoke with others (President Charles W. Eliot of Harvard University, Edward A. Filene, Henry Sterling and Daniel Davenport), at the Economic Club's dinner, Boston. Reported in the *Boston Daily Advertiser*, November 17, 1904. Source: Brandeis Papers, Box 233, pp. 85-86.

Brandeis spoke on employers' policies in contradistinction to the policies of trade unions.

1904, December 2.

Untitled. An address delivered before the Public School Association, Brighton, Mass. Reprinted in Brandeis Univ. Document 28. There is a typed version in the Brandeis Papers, Box 233, pp. 211-213.

The topic was the need of citizens to vote at the then upcoming school committeemen election.

1905, February 5.

"An Economic Exhortation to Organized Labor." (Sometimes it is listed as "Trade Unionism and Employers.") Delivered before the Boston Central Labor Union, at the Wells Memorial Hall, Boston. Reported in the *Boston Globe, Boston Post, Boston Herald*, and *Boston Transcript*, all on February 6, 1905. Printed in the *National Civic Federation Monthly Review*, 1:2, 11 (March 1905). Reprinted in Brandeis Univ. Documents 55-61, which reprints the newspaper accounts of the speech. Listed by Mersky; and U&L I:282-283.

1905, February 24.

"The Massachusetts System of Dealing With Public Franchises." Delivered at Cooper Union, New York City. Reprinted in Brandeis Univ. Document 23. Listed by Mersky; *Curse of Bigness*, 202; and U&L I:258. A typed version of this speech (13 pp.) is in the Brandeis Papers, Box 233, pp. 261-273.

1905, February.

"Saving Often Makes Waste." An address delivered in Boston. Excerpted under that title in *Collier's Weekly* 122(9): 78 (August 28, 1948). Listed by Mersky.

There is a copy of the speech in the University of Louisville Law Library's Brandeis Papers.

1905, March 30.

Untitled. An address similar to Brandeis' February 5th speech, "An Economic Exhortation to Organized Labor." delivered, this time, to the Boston Lodge of Machinists, #264, at Machinists' Hall, Boston. Reported in the *Boston Traveler*, March 31, 1905. Source: Brandeis Papers, Box 233, p. 100.

1905, April 10.

"The Relations Between Employers and Trade Unions." Address before the Economic Club of Providence, R.I. Reported in the *Providence Journal*, the *Providence Evening Bulletin*, and the *Providence Evening Telegram*, all on April 11, 1905; and *Daily Trade Record* (New York), April 17, 1905. Reprinted in Brandeis Univ. Document 62.

1905, April 18.

"The Relations Between Employers and Trade Unions." Address delivered before the Economic Club of Portland, Maine. Reported in the *Portland Daily Press*, April 19, 1905; and *Daily Eastern Argus*, April 19, 1905. Reprinted in Brandeis Univ. Document 63.

1905, April 25.

"Peace with Liberty." Delivered at the first meeting of the Industrial Economics Department of the National Civic Federation at the Park Avenue Hotel, New York City. Brandeis was one of many speakers. The *New York Times* (April 26, 1905) printed an account of the meeting. Listed by U&L 1:304.

1905, late April.

"The Desirable Industrial Peace." An address delivered at a dinner meeting of the Civic Federation of New England. Printed in the *National Civic Federation Monthly Review*, 2:16 (May 15, 1905). Reprinted in Brandeis Univ. Document 64.

1905, May 4.

"The Opportunity in the Law." Delivered before the Harvard Ethical Society at Phillips Brooks House, Cambridge, Mass. Printed in *American Law Review* 39:555–563 (1905); and *Harvard Bulletin*, May 10, 1905. Reprinted in *Business—A Profession*, 313–327; and Brandeis Univ. Document 32. Listed by U&L I:321–322.

The speech represents Brandeis' views on the ethics of the legal profession.

1905, May 8.

Untitled. An address opposing the granting of a franchise to the Boston Elevated Railway Company to construct an elevated road through the streets of Cambridge. Delivered before the Public Franchise League in Cambridge. Reported in the *Cambridge Tribune*, May 13, 1905. Reprinted in Brandeis Univ. Document 25.

1905, May 9.

"Industrial Cooperation." Delivered before the Filene Co-operative Association, at the Tremont Temple, Boston. Reported in *Filene Co-operative Association Echo*, May 1905. Reprinted in *Curse of Bigness*, 35–37; and Brandeis Univ. Documents 65 and 66. Listed in Mersky.

1905, June 14.

Untitled. An address delivered to the Massachusetts Medical Society, at the Mechanics Hall, Boston. Reported in the *Boston Herald* and *Boston Evening Transcript*, both June 14, 1905. Reprinted in Brandeis Univ. Document 29.

Brandeis spoke on the topic of graft and corruption in municipal life and doctors' duties as citizens.

1905, October 26.

"Life Insurance: The Abuses and the Remedies." Delivered before the Commercial Club of Boston. The subject of this speech was insurance companies and savings bank life insurance. The speech was reported in most of the Boston newspapers on the day. Was printed also as a pamphlet (27 pp.). Reprinted in *Business—A Profession*, 109–153; excerpted in *Social and Economic Views*, 349–353; and Brandeis Univ. Document 36 (date given is October 25). Listed by U&L I:363–363.

Brandeis was the counsel for the Protective Committee of Policy-Holders in the Equitable Life Assurance Society, which was organized on April 14, 1905.

1905, November 24.

A partisan speech given for Mr. Louis Frothingham. Delivered at a Jamaica Plain Citizens' Association meeting, Ward 22 of Boston. His speech was printed in the *Boston Transcript* and *Boston Daily Advertiser*, both November 27, 1905. Listed by U&L I:385–386.

Frothingham was seeking the nomination to be a candidate for the position of mayor of Boston.

1905, November 28.

"What Loyalty Demands." An address delivered before the New Century Club on the occasion of the 250th anniversary of the first Jewish settlement in the United States, Hotel Bellevue, Boston. A typed version of the speech (4 pp.) is in the Brandeis Papers, Box 235, pp. 1–4. Listed by U&L I:386–387.

1905, November 29.

A speech on the same topic as his November 28th speech, but given before the Roslindale Citizens' Association at Fairview Hotel. Reported in the *Boston News*, November 29, 1905.

1906, January 11.

"Hours of Labor." Being part of a panel address delivered at the first annual meeting of the New England Civic Federation at Revere House, Boston. Reported in the *Boston Globe* and *Boston Herald*. Reprinted in *Business—A*

Profession, 28–36; and Brandeis Univ. Document 67 (with date of February 1, 1906). Listed by Mersky; and U&L I:391 and 397.

In a letter, Brandeis referred to this speech as "On Hours of Labor." See U&L I:397.

1906, May 10.

"Life Insurance." Brandeis spoke as part of a panel discussion at the sixteenth annual dinner-discussion of the Economic Club of Boston, at the American House. Brandeis spoke from the public's standpoint. Reported in the *Boston Daily Advertiser*, May 11, 1906. Source: Brandeis Papers, Box 235, p. 231.

1906, Sometime before September 15th.

"Wage Earners' Life Insurance." Delivered before the New York State Bar Association, Albany, N.Y. This speech was based upon his article, "Wage Earners Life Insurance." *Collier's Weekly* 37(5): 16–17, 28, 30 (September 15, 1906). Reprinted in *Curse of Bigness*, 3–17; and Brandeis Univ. Document 35 (the reference is only to the periodical article).

Sometimes, the speech is referred to as "Savings Bank Life Insurance for Workingmen."

His paper was published as "Savings Bank Life Insurance for Wage Earners." *Albany Law Journal* 69:50–55 (1907). Reprinted in *Business—A Profession*, 160–187; and *Social and Economic Views*, 353–359. Listed by U&L I:485–486.

1908, February 11.

"The New England Transportation Monopoly." Delivered before the New England Dry Goods Association, Boston. Printed as a pamphlet, 15 pp., by the Massachusetts Anti-Merger League. Reprinted in *Business—A Profession*, 255–278; *Social and Economic Views*, 386–387, excerpted as "Scientific Management and Trusts"; and Brandeis Univ. Document 103. Listed by Drushal; and Mersky.

1910, October 1.

"Savings Bank Life Insurance in Massachusetts." Taken from an address Brandeis delivered at the Colonial Theatre in Pittsfield, Mass. Reprinted in *Business—A Profession*, 182–197. An expansion of this speech entitled "Successes of Savings Insurance" is reprinted in Brandeis Univ. Document 47. Listed by Mersky.

1910, December 9.

"Jews as a Priest People." An interview published in the *Jewish Advocate* (Boston), pp. 1, 8 (December 9, 1910). Reprinted in *Brandeis on Zionism*, 36, as "Sympathy for the Zionist Movement"; and De Haas, 151–154. Listed by Mersky.

Also, it was printed in the *American Hebrew*, December 10, 1910. Listed by Mersky; and ZAL.

This is Brandeis' first recorded statement on Zionism.

1911, January.

Interview published in *American Cloak and Suit Review*, 159 (January 1911). Reprinted in *Curse of Bigness*, 266. Listed by Mersky.

1911, February 14.

Untitled. An address delivered at the annual banquet of the National Cloak and Suit Buyers Association, at the Waldorf Hotel, New York City. Printed in *American Cloak and Suit Review*, 9-11 (February 15, 1911). Reprinted in Brandeis Univ. Document 74.

1911, March.

An interview on the Interstate Commerce Commission and freight rates. Published in *American Cloak and Suit Review*, 106 (March 1911). Reprinted in *Curse of Bigness*, 192-194. Listed by Mersky.

1911, March.

Untitled. An address. Published in the *American Cloak and Suit Review*, 188 (March 1911). Listed by Mersky; and *Curse of Bigness*, 96.

1911, March 27.

"The New Conception of Industrial Efficiency." Delivered before the Economic Club of New York. The *New York Times* (March 28, 1911) carried a long excerpt. Printed in *Journal of Accountancy* 12:35-43 (May 1911). Reprinted in Brandeis Univ. Document 78. Listed by Mersky; and U&L II:418.

1911, April 2.

"Organized Labor and Efficiency." Delivered before the Boston Central Labor Union. Printed in *Survey* 26:148-151 (April 22, 1911). Reprinted in *Business—A Profession*, 37-50; and Brandeis Univ. Document 79. Listed by Drushal; and U&L II:418-419.

1911, June 8.

"The Workingmen's Insurance: The Road to Social Efficiency." Delivered before the National Congress of Charities and Correction, at the Tremont Temple, Boston. Printed in *The Outlook* 98:291-294 (June 10, 1911). Reprinted in *Business—A Profession*, 51-64, as "The Road to Social Efficiency"; *Social and Economic Views*, 369-370, excerpted as "Industrial Democracy"; and Brandeis Univ. Document 76. Listed by Drushal, as "The Road to Social Efficiency"; Mersky (but not as a speech); and U&L II:433-434.

1911, December 31.

"Menace of Trusts to Labor as Seen by Mr. Brandeis." An interview with Percy White of the *Boston Sunday Post*, December 31, 1911. Reprinted in Brandeis Univ. Document 132.

1912, January.

"The Roll Call: On Man and Measures." An address given before progressive businessmen in the Grand Pacific Hotel, Chicago. Printed in the *La Follette's Magazine*, 4(4): 4-5 January 27 and 4(5): 4-5 February 3, 1912. Reprinted in Brandeis Univ. Document 135, as "Protect Law Abiding Business."

1912, January 13.

Untitled. An address given at the New York Republican Club. Brandeis strongly attacked United States Steel's labor policy. Reported in the *New York Times*, January 14, 1912. Listed by U&L II:545-546.

1912, February 9.

"Big Business and Industrial Liberty." Delivered at the Ethical Culture Center, New York City. Reported in the *New York Times*, February 10, 1912. Listed by U&L II:545.

1912, February 10.

"Big Business and Industrial Liberty." Given at the Ethical Culture House, Boston. Printed in the *New York Times*, February 11, 1912. Reprinted in *Curse of Bigness*, 38-39; and Brandeis Univ. Document 137. Listed by Durshal; and Mersky.

1912, April 6.

Interview on the "Preferential Shop" which appeared in the *Boston Transcript* of this date. Reprinted in Brandeis Univ. Document 83.

1912, June 19.

"Business—A Profession." Delivered as the commencement address at Brown University. Printed in *System* 22:365-369 (October 1912) as "Business—The New Profession." Reprinted in *Business—A Profession*, 1-12; *Social and Economic Views*, 387-388, excerpted as "The Profession of Business"; and Brandeis Univ. Document 133. Listed by Drushal, as 1911, and U&L II:702.

Sometimes, the word "New" is placed before the word "Profession" in the speech's title.

1912, September 12.

"Third Term Trust Scheme to Deceive Labor." Delivered in Boston as a political speech for Robert La Follette. Printed in the *Boston Post*, September 19, 1912. Listed by Mersky.

1912, September 19.

"Labor and the New Party." Brandeis spoke on the issue of labor and trusts at the convention of the Massachusetts State Branch of the Federation of Labor, Fitchburg, Mass. Printed in *La Follette's Magazine* 4(41): 6-8, 19-22 (October 12, 1912). Reprinted in Brandeis Univ. Document 145. Listed by U&L II:673 and 676.

1912, October.

Brandeis wrote his brother, Alfred, on September 15th, saying he would spend most of the month of October speaking on the subject of trusts in the North Eastern portion of the United States before economic clubs, chambers of commerce, and similar groups. Source: U&L II:673.

In a letter dated October 2nd to William Gibbs McAdoo, Brandeis set out his October itinerary. See U&L II:697–698.

1912, October 7.

"Efficiency and the Trusts." Address delivered before the Providence Town Criers at Churchill House, Providence, R.I. This address was given also at the City Club of Rochester, N.Y. on October 12th, and before the Cleveland, Ohio Chamber of Commerce on October 15th. Reprinted in Brandeis Univ. Document 142A.

Brandeis' speech was advertised as dealing with the commercial and social bearing of scientific management, or the efficiency ideal.

1912, October 10.

Untitled. An address given before a Y.M.C.A. meeting in New York City on the topic of trusts, which Brandeis criticized as inefficient. Listed by U&L II:702.

1912, October 12. See October 7, 1912 entry.

1912, October 15.

Untitled. "Efficiency and Trusts." An address delivered before the Chamber of Commerce, Cleveland, Ohio. Was printed in *Manufacturers' News* of the Illinois Manufacturers' Association as "Men Should Be Higher Than Capital." October 24, 1912 issue. Listed by U&L II:703.

1912, November 1.

"The Regulation of Competition Against the Regulation Monopoly." Delivered at the Economic Club, Boston. Reprinted in *Curse of Bigness*, 109–111. Listed by Drushal.

1913, January 27.

"An Unusual Man of Law." An interview printed in the *New York Times Annalist* I(2): 36 (January 27, 1913). Reprinted in *Curse of Bigness*, 40–42. Listed by Mersky.

1913, March 20.

Untitled. An address delivered at the Plymouth Theatre, Boston at a reception (mass meeting) for Nahum Sokolow. Brandeis introduced him. Was printed later as a pamphlet. Reprinted as an excerpt in De Haas, 154–155, as "Acceptance of Zionism"; *Brandeis on Zionism*, 37–38, as "A Great Vision." Listed by Drushal (untitled); Harris, as "Acceptance of Zionism"; and Mersky (untitled).

Sokolow (1859–1936) was a noted Polish Jewish writer and linguist. Later, he became president of the World Zionist Organization.

The date of this speech is sometimes given as March 30th.

1913, May 14.

"On Maintaining Makers' Prices." Delivered before the annual banquet of the Association of National Advertising Managers, Hotel Astor, New York City. This speech was printed together with portions of Brandeis' testimony given before the United States House of Representatives' Committee on Patents in May 1912, in *Harper's Weekly* 57: 6 (June 14, 1913); and published as a pamphlet. Reprinted in *Curse of Bigness*, 125–128; and Brandeis Univ. Document 148. Listed by Drushal; and Mersky (but not as a speech); and U&L III:89.

Brandeis spoke as part of a panel discussion with Henry B. Joy, then president of the Packard Motor Car Company, on the topic of price maintenance.

1913, May 18.

Untitled. An address delivered before the Chelsea, Mass. Young Men's Hebrew Association. Reprinted in De Haas 155–159, as "We Cannot Afford to Do A Mean Thing"; *New York Jewish Review*, September 9, 1943; and *Brandeis on Zionism*, 39–42, as "To Be A Jew." Listed by Drushal (untitled); Harris, as "We Can Not Afford to do a Mean Thing"; Mersky; and ZAL.

1913, May 24.

"Brandeis on the Labor Problem: How Far Have We Come on the Road to Industrial Democracy?" An interview conducted by Treadwell Cleveland which was printed in *La Follette's Magazine* 5(21): 5–14 (May 24, 1913). Reprinted in *Curse of Bigness*, 43–47, as "How Far Have We Come on the Road to Industrial Democracy?"; and Brandeis Univ. Document 87. Listed by Mersky.

1913, May 28.

Untitled. An address given before the annual meeting of the Federation of Jewish Charities held at Temple Israel, Boston. On short notice Brandeis replaced Edward A. Filene. The speech was reported in the *Boston Post*, May 29, 1913; and *Jewish Advocate*, May 30, 1913. Source: Brandeis Papers, Box 235, pp. 26–28.

1913, June 11.

"Price Fixing." An address given before the Associated Advertising Clubs of America at its convention in Baltimore, Maryland. There is a typed version of the speech, 8 pp., in the Brandeis Papers, Box 235, pp. 316–323.

The speech may have been typed after it was given, as it concludes "Great Applause."

1913, December 2.

A three-hour conversation privately held at the University Club, New York City, between Brandeis and Thomas W. Lamont, a partner in J. P. Morgan & Company, with Norman Hapgood present to record their views. It was published in *Business History Review* 47:72–94 (1973) (See chapter 5, *infra* under Abrahams). Reprinted in Brandeis Univ. Document 162.

1913, December 15.

"The World May Be Fooling Itself." An interview printed in the *New York Times Annalist*, II(48): 740 (December 15, 1913). Reprinted in Brandeis Univ. Document 151. Listed by Mersky.

1914, February 5.

"The Democracy of Business." Delivered before the Chamber of Commerce of the United States at its second annual meeting in Washington, D.C., Also printed as a pamphlet. Reprinted in *Curse of Bigness*, 137–142; and Brandeis Univ. Document 166. Listed by Drushal; and Mersky.

1914, August 30.

Acceptance of the chairmanship of the Zionist Provisional Emergency Committee, at the Hotel Marseilles, New York. Reprinted in De Haas, 161–162; and *Brandeis on Zionism*, 43–45, as "The Jewish People Should Be Preserved." Listed by Harris; Mersky; and ZAL.

1914, September.

Untitled. "A Message to American Zionists." Not a speech. Reprinted in *Brandeis on Zionism*, 46–48, as "Strain Every Nerve." Listed by ZAL.

This is Brandeis' first official statement after becoming chairman of the Zionist Provisional Emergency Committee.

1914, October 4, on or before.

"The Rebirth of the Jewish Nation." Delivered at Symphony Hall, Boston. Printed in full in the *Boston American*, October 4, 1914. Reprinted in De Haas, 163–170; *Brandeis on Zionism*, 49–58, excerpted as "The Fruits of Zionism"; and in *Curse of Bigness*, 209–217, as "Zionism and Patriotism." Listed by Drushal; Harris (used the date September 27); and Mersky.

The Federation of American Zionists issued the speech in an expanded version under the title, "Zionism and Patriotism."

1914, October 25.

"Why I Am A Zionist." An address given at the Free Synogogue, New York City. Listed by Harris; and U&L III:308–309.

1914, November 8.

"A Call to the Educated Jew." Delivered at the Conference of the Inter-Collegiate Menorah Association, New York. Printed in *The Menorah Journal* 1:13–19 (January 1915). Reprinted in De Haas, 190–200; as a pamphlet by the

Zionist Organization of America, Department of Youth and Education (1941); *Brandeis on Zionism*, 59–69, in an abridged format; and *Zionist Lawyer* 6:4–8 (November 1948). Listed by Drushal (with the date January 1915); Harris, as "Duty of Educated Jews"; Mersky (but not as a speech); and ZAL (used date of 1916).

1914, November 13.
    "Interlocking Directorates." Delivered before the American Academy of Political and Social Science, Philadelphia. Printed in its *Annals* 57:45–49 (January 1915). Reprinted in *Business—A Profession*, 320–328; and Brandeis Univ. Document 33. Listed by Drushal (used date of January 1915); Mersky (but not as a speech); and U&L V:536.
    Brandeis spoke on a panel entitled, "Practical Utility Problems."

1914, November 22.
    Untitled. Listed by Harris as "The Jewish Future Can Be as Secure as the Past."

1914, December 9.
    "Constructive Co-operation vs. Cut-Throat Competition." Delivered before the National Rivers and Harbors Congress. Washington, D.C. Printed in *Harper's Weekly* 60:573–574 June 12, 1915), as "Co-operation vs. Cut-Throat Competition." Reprinted in *Curse of Bigness*, 195–201; and Brandeis Univ. Document 169. Listed by Drushal; Mersky (but not as a speech); and U&L V:536.

1914–1915.
    Untitled. Excerpts of several addresses Brandeis delivered during 1914–1915 on behalf of the Funds of the Zionist Provisional Emergency Committee. Reprinted in *Brandeis on Zionism*, 49–58, excerpted as "The Fruits of Zionism." Listed by ZAL. See also October 4, 1914 entry.

1915.
    "Zionism and Palestine." See October, 1914 entry, "The Rebirth of the Jewish Nation."

1915, January. See November 13, 1914 entry.

1915, February 8.
    "An Essential of Lasting Peace." An address given before the Economic Club of Boston. Published in *Harper's Weekly* 60:259 (March 13, 1915); and *National Economic League Quarterly* 1:24–26 (May 1915). Reprinted in *Curse of Bigness*, 267–269. Listed by Drushal; and U&L III:436.

1915, February 14.
    Interview in the *Boston Post* of this date regarding John D. Rockefeller's testimony before the United States Commission on Industrial Relations. Source: Brandeis Papers, Box 234, pp. 308–309.

1915, April 6.

"Twin Evils of Literacy Test." An address on immigration delivered at the New Century Club of Boston's banquet for the New England Congressmen who sustained President Woodrow Wilson's veto of a bill requiring a literacy test for immigrants. Printed in *La Follette's Magazine* 7(4): 8 (April 1915). Listed by U&L III:506.

1915, April 11.

Untitled. Listed by Harris, as "Zionist Work of the Free Synagogue Has Been Great."

1915, April 12.

"The Organization of American Israel." Listed by Harris.

1915, April 25.

"The Jewish Problem and the Organization of Israel." Listed by Harris.

1915, May 2.

"Group Liberty." Delivered before the Collegiate Zionist Society of Columbia University, New York City. Reprinted in *Brandeis on Zionism*, 70, as an excerpt, Listed by ZAL.

1915, June.

"The Jewish Problem: How to Solve It." Delivered before the Eastern Council of Reform Rabbis. Reprinted as a pamphlet many times since. De Haas, 170–190; *Curse of Bigness*, 218–232; and *Brandeis on Zionism*, 12–35. Listed by Drushal; Mersky; U&L III:455; and ZAL.

1915, June 26–28.

Brandeis gave several speeches before the Boston Zionist Convention in late June. Listed either grouped or individually by Drushal; Harris; Mersky; and ZAL. Below is a breakdown of them.

1915, June.

"American Aid." Reprinted in *Brandeis on Zionism*, 73–74. Listed by Harris (as June 27).

1915, June.

"Dreams May Be Made Into Realities." Reprinted in *Brandeis on Zionism*, 71–72; Listed by Harris, as "The Zionist Dream Can Become a Reality" (as June 27).

1915, June.

"Every Jew a Zionist." Reprinted in *Brandeis on Zionism*, 76–79.

1915, June.

"A Testimony of Faith." Delivered at an open-air session of Zionist Convention, Chelsea, Mass. Reprinted in De Haas, 200–206. Listed by Drushal.

1915, June.
"The Zionist Movement is Democratic." Reprinted in *Brandeis on Zionism*, 75–76.

1915, July 5.
"True Americanism." A Fourth of July oration delivered at Faneuil Hall, Boston. Printed in *Harper's Weekly* 61:31–32 (July 10, 1915. Has been printed often as a pamphlet, 8 pp. Reprinted in *Business—A Profession*, 364–374; *Brandeis on Zionism*, 3–11; and Brandeis Univ. Document 176. Listed by Drushal; Mersky; and U&L III:540.

The word "oration" is used on the cover of the pamphlet. The speech was given on July 5th, a Monday. Sometimes July 4th is used as the date of the speech.

1915, September 5.
Untitled. Listed by Harris, as "The Young Men's Hebrew Association Should Support Zionism."

1915, September 24.
"Forward to the Land." Listed by Harris.

1915, September 27.
"Jewish Unity and the Congress." Delivered before the Jewish Congress Organization Committee at the Opera House, Baltimore, Maryland. There is a 6-page transcript in the American Jewish Archives' Brandeis Near-Print File. Reprinted in *Curse of Bigness*, 233–237. Listed by Drushal; Mersky; and U&L III:675–676.

1915, October 17.
"Zionism and the Aims of Jewish Democracy." Listed by Harris.

1915, October 22.
"Efficiency by Consent." Delivered at the memorial meeting for Frederick W. Taylor, Philadelphia. Printed in *Harper's Weekly* 61:568 (December 11, 1915). Reprinted in *Business—A Profession*, 51–56; and *Social and Economic Views*, 410. Listed by Drushal; Mersky (but not as a speech); and U&L III:618.

1915, November.
"Democracy in Palestine." An address delivered in Washington, D.C. Printed in *The Independent* 84:311 (November 22, 1915). Reprinted in *Curse of Bigness*, 238–245, as "Palestine and Jewish Democracy." Listed by Drushal; Mersky (but not as a speech); and ZAL.

Most of this speech was included in Brandeis' article "Palestine and the Jewish Democracy." *The Outlook* 112:36–40 (January 5, 1916). Reprinted in *Curse of Bigness*, 238–245.

1915, December.

"The Victory of the Maccabees." A Chanukah message delivered to the Zionists of America. Not a speech. Reprinted in *Brandeis on Zionism*, 82-83. Listed by ZAL.

1915, December 1.

A Message to the Zionist Council of Greater New York on the occasion of its tenth anniversary celebration. Not a speech. Reprinted in *Brandeis on Zionism*, 80-81, as "Numbers Count." Listed by ZAL.

1916, n.d.

An address delivered at a conference of Menorah Societies. Listed by ZAL. See November 8, 1914 entry.

1916, January 2.

"Not By Charity Alone." Delivered before the Convention of the Knights of Zion (a Zionist organization) in Chicago. Reprinted as an excerpt in *Brandeis on Zionism*, 84-88. Listed by ZAL.

1916, January 3.

"The Living Law." Delivered before the Chicago Bar Association. Printed in *Illinois Law Review* 10:461-471 (1916) and in *Harper's Weekly* 62:173-174 and 201-202 (February 19 and 26, 1916). Reprinted in *Business—A Profession*, 344-363; *Curse of Bigness*, 316-326; and Brandeis Univ. Document 99. Listed by Drushal.

1916, January 22.

"Brandeis on Coupon Evil." An interview with Roy Atkinson of the *Boston Post*, January 22, 1916. Listed by U&L IV:23.

1916, January 24.

"Jewish Rights and the Congress." Delivered before the Jewish Congress Organization Committee, (mass meeting) Carnegie Hall, New York City. Has also been issued as a pamphlet, 11 pp. Reprinted in De Haas, 218-231, as "Jewish Rights"; and *Brandeis on Zionism*, 97-109, "The Common Cause of the Jewish People." Listed by Drushal, twice, once as above and once as "Common Cause of the Jewish People"; Mersky; and ZAL.

1916, July 2.

Untitled. Brief remarks delivered to the Provisional Zionist Emergency Committee, which met at the Federation of American Zionists' nineteenth annual convention, Philadelphia. Reprinted in *Brandeis on Zionism*, 89-90, as "Blackstone and Herzl." Listed by ZAL.

Rev. William A. Blackstone in 1891 urged the creation of a Jewish homeland. Blackstone may have spoken before Brandeis.

1916, July 2.

Untitled. Listed by Harris, as "The Jewish Nationality Can Continue to Grow and Develop." This may be the above entry.

1916, July 7.

"The Duties of Jewish Democracy." Delivered to the Provisional Zionist Emergency Committee, which met at the Federation of American Zionists' convention, Philadelphia. Reprinted in De Haas, 206–212; and *Brandeis on Zionism*, 91–96, as "Democracy Means Responsibility." Listed by Drushal; Harris; Mersky; and ZAL.

1916, July 16.

Untitled. An address on the topic of unity, given at the Hotel Astor, New York City, as reported in the *New York Tribune*, July 17, 1916. According to the article, Brandeis was hissed, scorned and rebuked by the audience. Source: Brandeis Papers, Box 235, p. 143.

1916, November 26.

Acknowledgement of a testimonial presented to Brandeis on his sixtieth birthday in the office of Nathan Straus, New York City. Not a speech. Reprinted in De Haas, 231–232; and *Brandeis on Zionism*, 110–111 as "Zionism Brings Understanding and Happiness." Listed by Mersky (used date of November 13); and ZAL.

1917, February 18.

"Members, Money and Discipline." A brief note to Morris Rothenberg, Chairman of the Zionist Council of Greater New York, as a letter of greetings. Not a speech. Reprinted in *Brandeis on Zionism*, 112. Listed by ZAL, as "Letter of Greeting."

1920, July 7.

"The Upbuilding of Palestine." Delivered at the opening meeting of the World Zionist Organization's conference in London. Reprinted in De Haas, 233–234; and *Brandeis on Zionism*, 113–115, as "The Time is Urgent." Listed by Harris; Mersky; and ZAL.

The London Conference lasted from July 7th through the 22nd.

1920, July 14.

"Reorganization Plan." Delivered before the American Delegation of the World Zionist Organization in London. Reprinted in De Haas, 241–259; and *Brandeis on Zionism*, 116–125, excerpted as "Efficiency in Public Service." Listed by Harris; and Mersky.

1920, July 14.

Untitled. Brandeis gave this speech in London when he accepted the honorary presidency of the World Zionist Organization. There is a 7-page

"Statement of Justice Brandeis to the American Delegation to the Zionist Conference at London" in the American Jewish Archives, Brandeis Near-Print File. Listed by Harris.

1920, July 19.
   Untitled. "An Alternative Plan is Necessary." Listed by Harris.

1920, July 20.
   Untitled. "American Zionists Must Refuse Any World Leadership." Listed by Harris.

1920, August 24.
   "The *Zeeland* Memorandum." Written by Brandeis on board the S.S. Zeeland, while returning to the United States from the World Zionist Organization's Conference. Not a speech. Reprinted in De Haas, 260–272; and *Curse of Bigness*, 246–254. Listed by Mersky.

1920, August 29.
   "Review of the London Conference." Delivered before the National Executive Committee of the American Zionist Organization in New York City. Reprinted in De Haas, 234–241. Listed by Harris; and Mersky.

1921, June 10.
   "Social Economic Policy." Delivered at the office of Nathan Straus before the supporters of the economic development of Palestine, New York City. Reprinted in De Haas, 273–278. Listed by Harris; and Mersky.

1923, May 27.
   "Confidence in Palestine." Delivered before the second annual conference of the Palestine Development Council and of the Palestine Development Leagues, New York City. Reprinted in De Haas, 278–285; and *Brandeis on Zionism*, 126–133, as "The Pilgrims Had Faith." Listed by Harris; Mersky; and ZAL.

1923, May 28.
   "Men as Natural Resources." Delivered before the second annual conference of the Palestine Development Council and of the Palestine Development Leagues, New York City. Reprinted in De Haas, 285–286; and *Brandeis on Zionism*, 134–135, as "The Human Resource." Listed by Harris; Mersky; and ZAL.

1923, June 24.
   "Taking the Initiative in Palestine." Delivered before the Palestine Development League, Boston. Reprinted in De Haas, 286–292; and *Brandeis on Zionism*, 136–142, as "Realization Will Not Come as a Gift." Listed by Harris; Merksy; and ZAL (as Summer 1923).

1923, September 6.
"Self-Help in Palestine." Delivered before the Palestine Development League, in the office of Nathan Straus, New York City. Reprinted in De Haas, 292–295. Listed by Harris; and Mersky.

1924, February 17.
"The Only Promising Road." A message to an all-day conference of Zionists and Non-Zionists, New York City. Not a speech. Reprinted in De Haas, 296, as "Palestine The Only Answer"; and *Brandeis on Zionism*, 143. Listed by Harris; and ZAL.

1924, June 28.
Untitled. An address delivered before the Elysium Club in Boston. Printed in *Jewish Advocate* of June 28, 1924.

1924, November 24.
Untitled. An address delivered at the first session of the Emergency Palestine Economy Conference (a protest conference), in Washington, D.C. Reported in the *New York Times*, November 25, 1929, p. 20. Reprinted in *Brandeis on Zionism*, 144–149, as "Palestine Has Developed Jewish Character"; and *Curse of Bigness*, 255–257. Listed by Harris, as "Success Is Open to Us Now"; Mersky; and ZAL.

1929, November 24.
"Jews and Arabs." Delivered at the launching of the Economic Cooperation for Palestine Organization, at the second session of the Emergency Palestine Economy Conference, Washington, D.C. Printed in *New Palestine* 14:454–455 (November 29, 1929), as "The Will To a Jewish Palestine, Success is Open to Us Now." Reprinted in *Brandeis on Zionism*, 150–153. Listed by Harris; Mersky; U&L V:413; and ZAL.

1930, June 30.
A Letter to the Zionist Organization of America's convention, Cleveland, Ohio. Not a speech. Listed by ZAL.

1931, November 9.
Acknowledgement of seventy-fifth birthday greetings from the thirty-fourth annual convention of the Zionist Organization of America in Atlantic City, N.J. Not a speech. Reprinted in *Brandeis on Zionism*, 154, as "A Zionist's Vow." Listed by ZAL.

1939, May 18.
"Jews Will Continue to Enter Palestine." A statement presented by Justice Brandeis through Dr. Solomon Goldman, then president of the Zionist Organization of America. The statement was given in reference to Great Britain's "White Paper" limiting the immigration of Jews to Palestine. Reprinted in *Brandeis on Zionism*, 155–156. Listed by ZAL.

CHAPTER 8

Speeches about Brandeis

This chapter consists of speeches that have not been fully reprinted in a printed form, or not printed at all.

Baker, Leonard. "Louis Brandeis: The Jew and the American Liberal Tradition." Being the third annual Israel Naamani Memorial Lecture, given on March 25, 1982 at the University of Louisville.

Baldwin, Roger N. "Justice Brandeis and the Bill of Rights." A speech given at the October 2, 1966 Herzl Institute's "In Recall of Greatness" meeting. An excerpt of the speech appears in *Herzl Institute Bulletin* 3(5):1 (October 30, 1966).

Berman, Hyman. "The Awakening of Brandeis' Jewish Consciousness." A speech given at Herzl Institute's Louis D. Brandeis Biographical Conference, on March 18, 1967 in New York City.

Brandeis University. "Program of Centennial Dinner and Centennial Convocation." Program for a dinner in Waltham, Mass., November 11, 1956. At the dinner, remarks were made by Simon E. Sobeloff, Philip Grant Davidson, Jr., Calvert Magruder, Roscoe Pound, and Abram Leon Sachar. Most of the convocation was recorded.

Cohen, Benjamin Victor. (An Untitled Address.) Given at the Brandeis Centennial Dinner, New York City on October 22, 1956. There is a 6-page transcript of the speech in the Harvard Law Library.

Freund, Paul A. ". . . Brandeis, the Man and Philosopher." An address delivered at Temple Israel, St. Louis, Mo. on November 10, 1941. There is a 7-page typed version in the Harvard Law Library.

———, "Justice Brandeis In Today's World." Delivered at University of Louisville's convocation in commemoration of the centennial of the birth of Justice Louis Dembitz Brandeis, December 18, 1956, Louisville, Ky.

————, (An Untitled Speech.) A speech on Brandeis given at the thirtieth anniversary celebration of the founding of Brandeis University. Excerpts were printed in the *Boston Sunday Globe*, A4 (October 22, 1978).

Goldberg, Arthur J. (An Untitled Speech.) A speech given at the annual dinner of the American-Israel Public Affairs Committee, Washington, D.C. 1965. An excerpt was published in *Israel Digest* 8(8) (May 21, 1965).

Halpern, Benjamin. "Brandeis and the Balfour Declaration." A speech given at Herzl Institute's Louis D. Brandeis Biographical Conference on March 19, 1967 in New York City.

Herzl Institute (New York City). Louis D. Brandeis Biographical Conference, March 18 and 19, 1967. A separate entry has been made in this chapter for each of the sixteen speakers.

————, "In Recall of Greatness, Upon the Twenty-Fifth Anniversary of the Passing of Louis D. Brandeis." October 2, 1966. Three speeches (by Baldwin, Keating, and Tyler) were given. Dr. Emanuel Neumann presided. Each speech is listed herein.

Jacobs, Rose. "Brandeis and Hadassah." A speech given at Herzl Institute's Louis D. Brandeis Biographical Conference on March 19, 1967 in New York City. She was past-president of Hadassah.

Kallen, Horace M. "A Personal Memoir." A speech given at Herzl Institute's Louis D. Brandeis Biographical Conference on March 18, 1967 in New York City.

Keating, Kenneth B. "The Lawyer Statesman." A speech given at the October 2, 1966 Herzl Institute's "In Recall of Greatness" meeting. An excerpt of this speech appears in *Herzl Institute Bulletin* 3(5): 1 and 6 (October 30, 1966).

Kent, Raymond A. "Justice Brandeis as an Educator." Was delivered on the radio, over the Columbia Broadcasting System, November 13, 1938.

Landis, James. "Mr. Justice Brandeis." An address delivered at the tenth anniversary celebration of the Brandeis Youth Federation and the Brandeis Camp Institute on June 6, 1950, no location. A copy of the speech is in the Landis Papers, Library of Congress, Manuscript Division.

Landress, Sylvia. "Sources for Brandeis' Studies." A speech given at Herzl Institute's Louis D. Brandeis Biographical Conference on March 19, 1967 in New York City.

Louis D. Brandeis Biographical Conference, March 18 and 19, 1967 in New York City. See under Herzl Institute, *infra*.

Lowenthal, Marvin. "A Personality Profile of Louis D. Brandeis." A speech given at Herzl Institute's Louis D. Brandeis Biographical Conference on March 18, 1967 in New York City.

Magruder, Calvin. (An Untitled Speech.) Given at the annual convention of the New England Zionist Region in Boston(?) on June 3, 1956. There is a 5-page, typed copy in the Magruder Papers (File 33-7) in the Harvard Law Library's Manuscript Division. Magruder was Brandeis' first law clerk.

———, (An Untitled Speech.) Given at Temple Israel, Boston, no date. There is a 15-page typed copy in the Magruder Papers (File 33-9) in the Harvard Law Library's Manuscript Division.

Margulies, Morris. "A Personal Memoir." A speech given at Herzl Institute's Louis D. Brandeis Biographical Conference on March 19, 1967 in New York City.

Panitz, Esther. "Brandeis and the Cleveland Conference." A speech given at Herzl Institute's Louis D. Brandeis Biographical Conference on March 19, 1967 in New York City.

Parzen, Herbert. "Brandeis and the Unification Effort within the Z.O.A. Leadership of the Late Twenties." A speech given at Herzl Institute's Louis D. Brandeis Biographical Conference on March 19, 1967 in New York City.

Payer, Harry F. "Louis D. Brandeis, Jurist and Humanitarian." An address delivered on Sunday, December 6, 1936 at Mahler Hall, the Ansel and East 105th Temple, Atlantic City, N.J. There is a 15-page typed copy in the Harvard Law Library.

Richards, Bernard G. "A Personal Memoir." Given at Herzl Institute's Louis D. Brandeis Biographical Conference on March 19, 1967 in New York City.

Ronall, Joachim O. "Brandeis and His Economic Effort in Palestine." A speech given at Herzl Institute's Louis D. Brandeis Biographical Conference on March 19, 1967 in New York City.

Rudavsky, David. "Brandeis at the London Conference." A speech given at Herzl Institute's Louis D. Brandeis Biographical Conference on March 19, 1967 in New York City.

Schenker, Avram. "Brandeis and the First American Kibbutz (Ein Hashofet)." A speech given at Herzl Institute's Louis D. Brandeis Biographical Conference on March 19, 1967 in New York City. There is a 29-page typed version of text plus 7 pages of footnotes in the Zionist Archives and Library, New York City. The kibbutz was organized in 1938.

Sherman, C. Bezalel. "Brandeis and the American Jewish Congress." A speech given at Herzl Institute's Louis D. Brandeis Biographical Conference on March 19, 1967 in New York City.

Shubow, Leo. "The Beginnings of Brandeis' Zionism." A speech given at Herzl Institute's Louis D. Brandeis Biographical Conference on March 19, 1967 in New York City.

Strum, Phillippa. "Brandeis and the Exercise of Judicial Power." Being a paper delivered at the annual meeting of the American Political Science Association in Washington, D.C., September 1–4, 1977. The University of Louisville Law Library has a printed copy of the speech, 37 pages of text and 20 pages of footnotes.

Szajkowski, Zosa. "Brandeis and Jewish Relief." A speech given at Herzl Institute's Louis D. Brandeis Biographical Conference on March 19, 1967 in New York City.

Szold, Robert. "Brandeis as a Spiritual Force Today." Being the Commencement Address given at the College of Jewish Studies, on June 14, 1959. There is a photocopied, 13-page, typed version (in poor condition) in the Zionist Archives and Library, New York City.

Tyler, Gus, "Louis D. Brandeis' Way to Jewish Identification." A speech given at the October 2, 1966's Herzl Institute's "In Recall of Greatness" meeting. An excerpt of his speech appears in *Herzl Institute Bulletin* 3(6): 1, 2 and 6 (November 6, 1966).

Urofsky, Melvin I. "Louis D. Brandeis and American Zionism: Politics and Religion." Is a paper he presented at the American Academy of Religion on October 25, 1969 at Newton, Mass.

CHAPTER 9

Miscellany

Brandeis, Louis D. *Eight Pages from the Circuit Court of the City of St. Louis, 1878–1879, Representing Cases of Louis Dembitz Brandeis.* 8 parts in 1 vol. This item is located in the Treasure Room, Harvard Law Library.

Frankfurter, Felix. *Mr. Justice Brandeis.* 9-page typescript. Located in File 02662 of the Felix Frankfurter Papers, Manuscript Division, Library of Congress, Washington, D.C.

A curtailed version of this article was published in the *New York Times Magazine* of November 11, 1956 under the title, "Moral Grandeur of Justice Brandeis."

Riesman, David. *Notes for an Essay on Justice Brandeis.* An unpublished letter to Felix Frankfurter, dated May 22, 1936. There is a typed transcript (5 pp.) in the Felix Frankfurter Papers, Manuscript Division, Library of Congress, Washington, D.C.

Professor Riesman was one of Brandeis' law clerks and is quite critical of Brandeis.

The Zionist Organization of America issued a series of mimeographed articles on the Justice. Probably these articles were issued as memorials to the Justice. I found four of them in the Zionist Archives and Library's vertical file. Their physical condition is terrible, close to disintegration. They are:

Lowenthal, Marvin. *Brandeis at the Zionist Convention of 1915.* 3 pp. October 17, 1941 (ZR 133).

Goldman, Solomon. *His Character—the Arbitrar of His Destiny.* 5 pp., (October 15, 1941 (ZR 129).

Gebber, N. M. *The Role Which Justice Brandeis Played in Winning President Wilson Over to Zionism.* 5 pp. n.d., n.n.

De Haas, Jacob. *Brandeis as Zionist*. 3 pp. n.d. (ZR 127).

Justice Brandeis was on the cover of at least three issues of *Time Magazine*: 5(16), (October 19, 1925) (just showing his head); 16(1), (July 7, 1930) (a head and shoulders portrait, with Brandeis wearing a robe), with a story in the Religion Section; and 30(20), (November 15, 1937) (a full-length portrait, a serious-looking Brandeis, wearing a suit and facing left), with a story in the National Affairs Section.

NON-BOOK MATERIALS

Lawyer from Boston, a 30-minute film, Kinescope series of NBC-TV Religious Hour Program. Produced by the Jewish Theological Seminary of America, New York City.

Louis D. Brandeis: Giant of Justice and Champion of Zion. a 42-frame, in color, filmstrip created in 1966 by the Department of Education and Culture of the Jewish Agency (New York City). It was produced for senior high school students and adults. It is the fourth in its series of color filmstrips entitled *Dreams and Builders of Zion*.

To Live by That Heritage. A 31-frame, black and white filmstrip, prepared under the editorial auspices of the Theodor Herzl Institute (New York City) by Millard Lampell in 1957. It is an imaginery interview with Justice Brandeis, created for intermediate and junior high school students. Lampell also produced an 8-page booklet to accompany the filmstrip.

Brandeis. The Eternal Light radio program, chapter 254. January 15, 1950. 30 mins. in length. There is a radio script of the broadcast.

The Columbia Broadcasting System devoted a half-hour of radio time (5:00 to 5:30 p.m. EST) on Sunday, November 13, 1938 to honor Brandeis on the occasion of his eighty-second birthday. The main speakers were Neville Miller, former dean of the University of Louisville Law School and then president of the National Association of Broadcasters, who discussed Brandeis as an individual; and Raymond A. Kent, president of the University of Louisville, whose address is entitled "Justice Brandeis as an Educator."

Also paying tribute to the Justice were President Franklin Delano Roosevelt (Dr. Kent read his message), federal Judge Learned Hand and Professor Alpheus T. Mason (Brandeis' biographer), who elaborated on Brandeis' humanitarian traits. The *New York Times* (November 14, 1938, p. 14) contains a story on the broadcast.

There does not seem to be any sound recording of Justice Brandeis' voice or him delivering a speech. The Jewish Museum's National

Jewish Archive of Broadcasting (New York City) has not indicated to me that they own any.

Strangely, there do not seem to be any recorded comments by Brandeis on the horrible Triangle Shirtwaist Company fire in 1911 in New York City where 145 young girls died.

In observance of the one hundredth anniversary of Brandeis' birth, in 1956, the United States Mint at Philadelphia struck 3,000 bronze medallions. They were first distributed at the Brandeis Centennial Dinner at Brandeis University (November 11, 1956) and then sold at the campus bookstore.

The design was the idea of Emanuel M. Gilbert, Director of Public Affairs of Brandeis University. The medallion was executed by the sculptor-engravers at the Mint.

S.S. *Louis D. Brandeis,* a 10,000-ton Liberty Ship, was launched at the Bethlehem-Farfield Shipyard, Baltimore, Md., on February 20, 1943. His daughter, Susan Brandeis Gilbert, smashed the traditional champagne bottle across the vessel's prow to launch it. The *New York Times* printed a very short story on the ceremony (February 21, 1943, p. 35, col. 6).

In 1960, the P. Lorillard Company issued the following advertisement honoring Brandeis.

The law must still protect a man...

"*The law must still protect a man from things that rob him of his freedom, whether the oppressing force be physical, or of a more subtle kind.*"

Thus spoke Louis Dembitz Brandeis who sat in the seats of the mighty when America needed a dozen Solomons. For in the years of crisis, when this country was fighting its way out of a great depression, his philosophical point of view as expressed from the Supreme Court bench helped to guide us to a rebirth of confidence and prosperity.

Louis Brandeis was born in Louisville, Kentucky in 1856, to parents who had fled from Bohemia during the revolution of 1848. After a distinguished law career

he was appointed to the Supreme Court by President Woodrow Wilson in 1916.

Here, for the next twenty-three years, he performed in a manner which will enshrine his name forever with America's great Justices. He was a man for the times. For he, better than many of his contemporaries, recognized the fact that a changing country needed—indeed, must have—new laws to fit the changing times.

It is to the eternal credit of Louis Brandeis that he, with Justice Oliver Wendell Holmes beside him, always insisted that the Supreme Court must not shackle with dogmas of the past, the legislative efforts to meet the public needs. "*The law must still protect a man ...*"

CHAPTER 10

Sources Used and Guide for Future Research on Justice Brandeis

I worked in the following libraries and used the sources listed herein in compiling this bibliography. In addition, I have detailed data and informational sources to aid those doing research on the Justice.

LIBRARIES IN WHICH I WORKED

Law Library
University of Louisville
Louisville, KY 40292

Besides having the major portion of the Brandeis Papers, the Law Library attempts to own every published book written about the Justice.

William F. Ekstrom Library
University of Louisville
Louisville, KY 40292

Louisville Free Public Library
Fourth and York Streets
Louisville, KY 40202

Its Kentucky Authors Scrap Book Collection contains four huge scrapbooks (Boxes 8 & 9) of clippings from various American newspapers on the Justice.

The Filson Club Library
1310 South 3rd Street
Louisville, KY 40208

Library
Indiana University—South East
New Albany, IN 47150

Jewish Room
New York Public Library
42nd Street and Fifth Avenue
New York, NY 10018

Library
YIVO Institute for Jewish Research
1048 Fifth Avenue
New York, NY 10028

Zionist Archives and Library
515 Park Avenue
New York, NY 10022

It owns many items on Brandeis that were issued in limited quantities, besides many letters written by Brandeis.

Brandeis University Library
Waltham, MA 02254

Law School Library
Harvard University
Cambridge, MA 02138

Its Manuscript Division contains the Brandeis Papers which cover the time period after he became a United States Supreme Court Justice, and the papers of several of his former law clerks.

Boston Public Library
666 Boylston Street
Boston, MA 02117

Manuscript Division
Library of Congress
Washington, D.C. 20540

Contains the Papers of Felix Frankfurter and James M. Landis. Moreover, Brandeis correspondence is in many persons' papers. Consult the Division's Indexes and Chapter 6, Correspondence . . . in Manuscript Collections, *infra.*

Law Library
Library of Congress
Washington, D.C. 20540

Hebrew Union College Library
3101 Clifton Avenue
Cincinnati, OH 45220

American Jewish Archives Library
3101 Clifton Avenue
Cincinnati, OH 45220

In addition to its holding of Brandeis letters, the Archives has an extensive collection of newspaper stories and articles on Brandeis in several folders, in its Near Print Files.

Its card catalog of manuscript holdings has been reproduced in book format by the G. K. Hall Company, 4 vols., 1971, and its first supplement, 1 vol., 1978.

Ohio State University Library
Columbus, OH 43210

PERIODICAL INDEXES

America: History and Life. Vol. 1 (1964/65) to vol. 23(3) (1986) paper issue.

American Jewish Archives (a periodical). Vols. 1 (1948) to 37 (1985).

> I consulted its annual indexes. The periodical contains articles on Brandeis and notices about Brandeis materials.

Bibliographic Index. Vol. 5 (1956-1959) to August 1986 paper issue.

Biography Index. Vol. 4 (1955-1958) to August 1986 paper issue.

Business Periodicals Index. Vol. 1 (July 1959) to October 1986 paper issue.

Current Law Index. Vol. 1 (1980) to August 1986 paper issue.

Dissertation Abstracts (Computer search).

Essay and General Literature Index. Vol. 5 (1955-1959) to June 1986 paper issue.

Humanities Index. Vol. 1 (1974-1975) to September 1986 paper issue.

Index to Canadian Legal Periodical Literature. 1961 to September 1985 paper issue.

> I did not locate any references to Justice Brandeis, however.

Index to Foreign Legal Periodicals. Vol. 1 (1060-1962) to 1985:2 paper issue.

Index to Jewish Periodicals. Vol. 1 (June 1963) to Vol. 22 (1-2) July–December 1984 paper issue.

Index to Legal Periodicals. Vol. 11 (1955-1958) to August 1986 paper issue.

Index to Periodical Articles Related to Law. (Merksy & Jacobstein, editors). Vol. 1 (1958) to Fall 1986 paper issue.

International Index. Vol. 14 (1955-1958) to vol. 18 (1964-1965) Ceased.

Palestine and Zionism. (Published by the Zionist Archives and Library of the Palestine Foundation Fund). Vol. 1 (1946) to vol. 11 (1956). Ceased.

Public Affairs Information Service Bulletin. Vol. 42 (1956) to September 1986 paper issue.

Readers' Guide to Periodical Literature. Vol. 20 (1955-1957) to October 25, 1986 paper issue.

Social Science Citations Index (Computer search).

Social Sciences and Humanities Index. Vol. 19 (1965-1966) to vol. 27 (1973-1974). Ceased. Continued *International Index.*

Social Sciences Index. Vol. 1 (1974-1975) to September 1986 paper issue.

BOOK BIBLIOGRAPHIES AND CATALOGS

Blandford, Linda, A., and Patricia Russell Evans, eds. *Supreme Court of the United States, 1789-1980: An Index to Opinions Arranged by Justice.* Sponsored by the Supreme Court Historical Society. 2 vols. Millwood, N.Y.: Kraus International Publications, 1983. Volume 1 covers 1789-1902; volume 2 covers 1902-1980.

Is arranged by justice in order of judicial appointment. Gives the citation to every opinion written by each justice for the Court, majority, concurring and dissenting opinions and in several miscellaneous categories. It is a great reference tool that will assist scholars to find all the opinions written by a specific justice. Hopefully will be updated in the future.

While I did not use this volume to compile this bibliography, it is an absolutely essential reference work for anyone wanting to research Brandeis' judicial decisions, which are listed in volume 2, pp. 629-645.

Cumulative Book Index. (C.B.I.) (New York: H. W. Wilson and Co.) 1953-1956 vol. to October 1986 paper issue.

DeVergie, Adrienne, and Mary Kate Kell, compilers. *Location Guide to the Manuscripts of Supreme Court Justices.* (Tarlton Law Library Legal Bibliography Series, no. 16) Austin: University of Texas Law Library. Sept. 1978. 146 pp.

They list twenty-nine collections of Brandeis Papers, pp. 8-10.

Hall, Kermit L. *A Comprehensive Bibliography of American Constitutional and Legal History, 1896-1979.* 5 vols. Millwood, N.Y.: Kraus International Publications, 1984. Vol. 5 is the index volume. The index is arranged by both author and subject.

There are several hundred entries under Brandeis as a subject. However, most of them are duplicates as Mr. Hall put the same article into various subject headings.

National Union Catalog of Manuscript Collections. Washington, D.C.: Library of Congress, 1959 (first volume) to date (1984).

Library of Congress. *Subject Catalog* (in book form). 1955 (first volume) to 1982.

Mersky, Roy. *Louis Dembitz Brandeis, 1856–1941: A Bibliography*. New Haven, Conn.: Yale Law School Library, 1958. 44 pp.

It is an indispensable reference tool for pre-1957 writings on Brandeis. Also, it contains a listing of Brandeis' speeches and writings. My bibliography supplements and updates Mersky's effort.

Stephenson, D. Grier, Jr. *The Supreme Court and the American Republic: An Annotated Bibliography*. New York: Garland Publishing Co., 1981, 281 pp.

Items 817 thru 831 (pp. 176–178) relate to Justice Brandeis.

U.S. National Historical Publications and Records Commission. *Directory of Archives and Manuscripts Repositories in the United States*. 1978 ed. Washington, D.C. The National Archives and Records Service. 905 pp.

U.S. National Historical Publications Commission. *A Guide to Archives and Manuscripts in the United States*. Edited by Philip M. Hamer. New Haven: Yale University Press, 1961. 775 pp.

Wigdor, Alexandra K. *The Personal Papers of Supreme Court Justices: A Descriptive Guide*. New York: Garland Publishing Co., Inc., 1986. 225 pp.

Four of the major repositories of Brandeis letters are described in some detail, at pp. 53–59. The four are: The American Jewish Archives, Brandeis University Library, The Harvard Law School Library, and the University of Louisville Law Library.

See also the indexes to the Brandeis Papers at Brandeis University, Harvard Law School and the University of Louisville, as to people associated with Brandeis, and the bibliographies, references and footnotes in the books and periodical articles, especially law reviews, on Brandeis (see *infra*).

INTERVIEWS AND ORAL HISTORY

The interviewing of contemporaries has become a major source of information in writing a biography. In chapter 1, I enumerate where in each biography the author listed his or her interviews, i.e., Allon Gal interviewed thirty-six people before writing his *Brandeis of Boston*.

Until the invention of the tape recorder, it was nearly impossible to quickly, accurately and completely record an individual's oral recollections about a person or event. The portable, battery-operated, lightweight tape and cassette recorder is a benefit to modern historians.

Modern oral history programs were pioneered by Columbia University's landmark effort. The Columbia University's Oral History Research Office's catalog in book format (*The Oral History Collection of Columbia University.* 3d ed. Edited by Elizabeth B. Mason and Louis M. Starr. 1973. 460 pp.) lists 2,697 people who were interviewed. After Columbia developed its formal, extensive project, other universities and groups followed its lead. For example, the University of Wisconsin operates an extensive oral history program. Professors William G. Rice, Jr. and J. Willard Hurst of its faculty, both former Brandeis law clerks, were interviewed; Rice did not discuss Brandeis, Hurst did.

It would be wonderful for scholars if some day one copy of all these taped oral history interviews concerning Justice Brandeis would be centralized in one locale, hopefully at the University of Louisville Law Library.

PEOPLE WHO WERE IN CONTACT WITH BRANDEIS

1. Presidents of the United States:

Woodrow Wilson, who appointed him to the United States Supreme Court. Before joining the Supreme Court, Brandeis advised him.

Franklin Delano Roosevelt, especially around the time of the court packing episode (1937).

2. Supreme Court Justices who sat with him:

Name	Years Served with Brandeis	Birth and Death Dates
Edward D. White Chief Justice	1916–1921	1845–1921
William H. Taft, Chief Justice	1921–1930	1857–1930
Charles E. Hughes, Chief Justice	1930–1939	1862–1948
Willis Van Devanter	1916–1937	1859–1941
Hugo L. Black	1937–1939	1886–1971
Oliver W. Holmes	1916–1932	1841–1935
Benjamin N. Cardozo	1932–1938	1870–1938
Felix Frankfurter	1939–1939	1882–1965
James C. McReynolds	1916–1939	1862–1946
William R. Day	1916–1922	1849–1923
Pierce Butler	1922–1939	1866–1939
John H. Clarke	1916–1922	1857–1945
George Sutherland	1922–1938	1862–1942
Stanley F. Reed	1938–1939	1884–1980
Mahlon Pitney	1916–1922	1858–1924
Edward T. Sanford	1923–1930	1865–1930
Owen J. Roberts	1930–1939	1875–1955
Joseph McKenna	1916–1925	1843–1926
Harlan F. Stone	1925–1939	1872–1946

3. His former law clerks:

Term of clerkship	Name, Dates, and Status
1916-1917	Calvert Magruder, 1893-1968. Deceased. Federal judge, First Circuit, U.S. Court of Appeals.
1917-1918 1918-1919	William A. Sutherland, 1896—. Attorney at law, Washington, D.C. Founder of Sutherland, Asbill & Brennan, Esqs.
1919-1920 1920-1921	Dean Acheson, 1893-1971. Deceased. U.S. Secretary of State, partner in Washington, D.C. law firm of Covington & Burling.
1921-1922	William G. Rice, Jr., 1892-1979. Deceased. Professor of Law, University of Wisconsin, Madison, Wisc.
1922-1923	William F. McCurdy, 1893-1967. Deceased. Professor of Law, Harvard University.
1923-1924	Samuel H. Maslon, 1901—. Partner in Minneapolis, Minn. law firm of Maslon, Edelman, Borman & Brand.
1924-1925	Warren S. Ege, 1901-1979. Deceased. Attorney at law, Washington, D.C.
1925-1926	James M. Landis, 1899-1964. Deceased. Attorney at law, expert in administrative law, and dean, Harvard Law School.
1926-1927	Robert G. Page, 1901-1970. Deceased. President of Phelps Dodge Corp., New York City.
1927-1928	Henry J. Friendly, 1903-1986. Deceased. Federal judge, Second Circuit, U.S. Court of Appeals, New York City.
1928-1929	Irving B. Goldsmith, 1902-1941. Deceased. Attorney at law, Chicago.
1929-1930	Harry Shulman, 1903-1955. Deceased. Dean, Yale Law School.
1930-1931	H. Thomas Austern, 1908-1984. Deceased. Partner in the Washington, D.C. law firm of Covington & Burling.
1931-1932	Henry M. Hart, Jr., 1904-1969. Deceased. Professor of Law, Harvard University.
1932-1933	Paul M. Freund, 1908—. Carl M. Loeb Professor of Law, Harvard University.
1933-1934	Louis A. Jaffe, 1905—. Professor of Law, Harvard University.
1934-1935	Nathaniel L. Nathanson, 1908-1983. Deceased. Professor of Law, Northwestern University, Chicago.
1935-1936	David Riesman Jr., 1909—. Professor of Sociology, Harvard University.
1936-1937	J. Willard Hurst, 1910—. Professor of Law, University of Wisconsin, Madison, Wisc.
1937-1938	W. Graham Clayton, Jr., 1912—. President of AMTRAK, Washington, D.C.
1938-1939	Adrian S. Fisher, 1914-1983. Deceased. Dean, Georgetown University Law Center, Washington, D.C. Negotiator of 1963 Limited (Nuclear) Test Ban Treaty.

4. American Zionist leaders, such as:

Julian J. Mack, Louis Marshall, Henrietta Szold, Robert Szold, Rabbi Stephen S. Wise, *et al.*

See especially chapter 6 of this bibliography, which shows the length and breadth of Brandeis' correspondence.

CONCEPTS WITH WHICH BRANDEIS WAS INVOLVED

1. *Administrative Law.* Brandeis greatly affected the development and direction that administrative law has taken by several means. He was one of the leaders of the reform movement, before he was nominated to the Supreme Court. Brandeis was one of the advocates for the creation of the Federal Trade Commission. His decisions while on the Supreme Court affected the administrative process and law, then and today.

For example, several of his law clerks have played important roles in shaping administrative law. Dean Acheson served as chairman of the 1941 Attorney General's Committee on Administrative Procedure. The Committee's final report is an enduring document that is constantly referred to. Law professors Henry Hart and Harry Shulman also served on the Committee.

Professor James Landis is ranked as one of the giants of administrative law because of his service with several federal administrative agencies, his writings and teaching. In addition to their teaching and scholarly writings, law professors Louis Jaffe and Nathaniel Nathanson edited an administrative law casebook, which has gone through several editions. The latest is the fourth edition, 1976, 1102 pp.

Federal Judge Henry Friendly's appellate decisions, out-of-court lectures and legal writings have impressed and influenced lawyers, law professors and fellow judges, due to his insights and clarity of thought.

2. *Balfour Declaration.* In 1917, Arthur Balfour (British Foreign Secretary), as a reward to Chaim Weizmann (a Russian émigré, Zionist, and a chemist who developed a process vital to the British war effort), stated that the British Government would create a Jewish homeland in Palestine under British rule. Besides sections in biographies of Brandeis, there are numerous non-legal periodical articles on this topic.

3. *Brief Writing (The Brandeis Brief).* The term "Brandeis Brief" is defined in *Black's Law Dictionary.* 5th ed. at p. 170 (see chap. 2, *infra*). His use of non-legal materials in his 1908 *Muller v. Oregon* brief revolutionized legal brief writing. Today it is standard procedure to

include more than legal arguments, references and authorities in briefs and in judicial opinions.

Law-related people understand what the words "Brandeis Brief" mean. For example, Professor Mark S. Pulliam uses the term as the first words of the title for his law review article, "Brandeis Brief For Decontrol of Land Use: A Plea For Constitutional Reform." *Southwestern University Law Review* 13:435 (1982-83).

4. *Economic Matters.* Both before and while on the Supreme Court, Brandeis played a critical role in the American economic and social reform movement. For example, he affected various topics such as,

Labor Reform Movement,
Savings Bank Life Insurance,
Scientific Management of Businesses,
The Railroad Industry,
Big Business and Monopolies, which he opposed.

5. *Erie Decision and Doctrine.* One of the most frequently cited American judicial decisions is *Erie Railroad Co. v. Tompkins*, 304 U.S. 64 (1938). Brandeis wrote the majority opinion. Briefly stated, in its simplest form, the *Erie* doctrine requires that in diversity of citizenship cases brought in federal courts, the federal judge must follow state law. The case has produced a gigantic amount of legal literature, i.e. Professor Charles Allan Wright devotes forty-seven pages to the doctrine in his civil procedure hornbook, *The Law of Federal Courts* (4th ed., St. Paul, Minn., 1983).

6. *Judaism.* Although not a practicing Jew, Brandeis ranks as the most prominent and visible American Jew in the first part of the twentieth century. He was active in the Zionist movement and was in contact with the other prominent American Jews of his era. His battle with Chaim Weizmann is still analyzed. Examine the wealth of non-legal periodical articles on this area of Brandeis' life.

7. *Privacy.* No discussion of the right of privacy begins without a reference to Warren and Brandeis' *Harvard Law Review* article on privacy (4:193-220, 1890). The right to be let alone is the reverse of the freedom of information doctrine. The article seems to have a life of its own. There are several law review articles devoted to *the article* itself (see chap. 2, *infra*).

8. *Zionism.* Although Brandeis did not accept the concept of a Jewish homeland until late in his life (in 1912) and was openly active in the Zionist movement only to 1920, his influence was great. See the huge and constant outpouring of non-legal periodical articles on Brandeis' role in the American Zionist movement. Also, consult the early records of various Zionist groups such as the Zionist Organization of America.